Company's Coming ®

DINNERS OF THE WORLD

by
Jean Paré

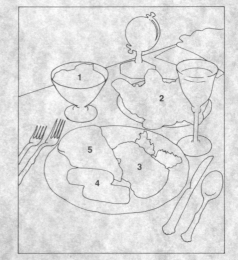

DINNERS OF THE WORLD

Second Printing September, 1991

I.S.B.N. 0-9693322-6-2

Published and Distributed by
Company's Coming Publishing Limited
Box 8037, Station "F"
Edmonton, Alberta, Canada
T6H 4N9

Printed in Canada

Cookbooks in the Company's Coming series by Jean Paré:

English Hard Cover Title

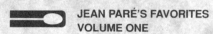

JEAN PARÉ'S FAVORITES
VOLUME ONE

English Soft Cover Titles

150 DELICIOUS SQUARES

COOKIES

CASSEROLES

VEGETABLES

MUFFINS & MORE

MAIN COURSES

SALADS

PASTA

APPETIZERS

CAKES

DESSERTS

BARBECUES

SOUPS & SANDWICHES

DINNERS OF THE WORLD

HOLIDAY ENTERTAINING

LUNCHES (April, 1992)

Cookbooks in the Jean Paré series:

French Soft Cover Titles

150 DÉLICIEUX CARRÉS

LES CASSEROLES

MUFFINS ET PLUS

table of Contents

Jean Paré was born and raised during the Great Depression in Irma, a small rural town in eastern Alberta, Canada. She grew up understanding that the combination of family, friends and home cooking is the essence of a good life. Jean learned from her mother, Ruby Elford, to appreciate good cooking and was encouraged by her father, Edward Elford, who praised even her earliest attempts. When she left home she took with her many acquired family recipes, her love of cooking and her intriguing desire to read recipe books like novels!

While raising a family of four, Jean was always busy in her kitchen preparing delicious, tasty treats and savory meals for family and friends of all ages. Her reputation flourished as the mom who would happily feed the neighborhood.

In 1963, when her children had all reached school age, Jean volunteered to cater to the 50th anniversary of the Vermilion School of Agriculture, now Lakeland College. Working out of her home, Jean prepared a dinner for over 1000 people which launched a flourishing catering operation that continued for over eighteen years. During that time she was provided with countless opportunities to test new ideas with immediate feedback – resulting in empty plates and contented customers! Whether preparing cocktail sandwiches for a house party or serving a hot meal for 1500 people, Jean Paré earned a reputation for good food, courteous service and reasonable prices.

"Why don't you write a cookbook?" Time and again, as requests for her recipes mounted, Jean was asked that question. Jean's response was to team up with her son Grant Lovig in the fall of 1980 to form Company's Coming Publishing Limited. April 14, 1981 marked the debut of "150 DELICIOUS SQUARES", the first Company's Coming cookbook in what soon would become Canada's most popular cookbook series. Jean released a new title each year for the first six years. The pace quickened and by 1987 the company had begun publishing two titles each year.

Jean Paré's operation has grown from the early days of working out of a spare bedroom in her home to operating a large and fully equipped test kitchen in Vermilion, Alberta, near the home she and her husband Larry built. Full time staff has grown steadily to include marketing personnel located in major cities across Canada plus selected U.S. markets. Home Office is located in Edmonton, Alberta where distribution, accounting and administration functions are headquartered in the company's own recently constructed 20,000 square foot facility. Company's Coming cookbooks are now distributed throughout Canada and the United States plus numerous overseas markets. Translation of the series to the Spanish and French languages began in 1990.

Jean Paré's approach to cooking has always called for easy-to-follow recipes using mostly common, affordable ingredients. Her wonderful collection of time-honored recipes, many of which are family heirlooms, is a welcome addition to any kitchen. That's why we say: taste the tradition.

Since the arrival of the jet age, an ever-growing number of people are visiting far-off places to enjoy different cultures. Television brings sights and sounds from around the world into our living rooms. Supermarkets and ethnic grocery stores shop the world on our behalf, sparking our taste for adventure.

This book is intended to help bring the world to your dinner table. Selected recipes from each course are offered from nine countries. From appetizers to desserts – follow the suggested menus provided or mix and match as you choose. Combine recipes from different countries for a unique multinational menu.

More main courses han other dishes have been included. This allows for more flexibility in choosing menus as vegetables and other side-dishes are easily interchanged. All recipes serve approximately eight people.

Invite Great Britain into your dining room with Beetroot Salad, Minted Peas and Yorkshire Pudding. Italy brings Osso Buco with Risotto Milanese and sensational Italian Cheesecake. Try Enchiladas from Mexico, Snow Eggs from France and Sauerkraut from Germany. A favorite from the United States is the fabulous Pacific Rim Salad. From China comes Red Tenderloin. Canada contributes Maple Syrup Pie to satisfy that sweet tooth.

I have made a real effort to adhere to my practise of producing "easy to follow recipes using mostly common affordable ingredients". In numerous cases I have adjusted the method or substituted ingredients to accommodate that need. Meanwhile, I have done my best to provide you with authentic-tasting recipes from each land.

I invite you to use this book as your ticket to kitchens around the globe.

So next time company's coming to your home, give them the world!

Jean Paré

 CANADA

From one rugged coastline to another, across vast expanses of prairie and arctic tundra, Canada's people enjoy culture as rich and varied as her landscape.

Canadian cuisine is affected by many peoples, but the historical influence of England and France is most evident. The English tradition of afternoon tea is still enjoyed in many Canadian hotels. Other Canadian restaurants rival those in France with their sensational presentations and gastronomical delights.

Even though cooking has become less regionalized over the years, French Canadians have retained much of their own style. Prairie menus tend to make the most of beef and pork and those from coastal regions naturally include more seafood dishes. Bread or dinner buns are standard with meals.

Wholesome flavorful meals await you at your Canadian table!

MENU 1

Shrimp Appetizer Page 9
Vinaigrette Salad Page 19
*Tourtière Québécoise Page 10 *or*
Seafood Casserole Page 11
Mashed Potatoes Page 16
Zucchini Patties Page 14 *or*
Carrot Coins Page 19
Saskatoon Pie Page 20
Coffee   Tea

MENU 2

Lobster and Shrimp Mold Page 12
Strawberry Greens Page 10
*Baked Salmon Page 13
Pacific Rice Page 15
Onion Casserole Page 14
*Maple Syrup Pie Page 21 *or*
Rhubarb Crisp Page 20
Coffee   Tea

*Pictured page 17

Making use of canned shrimp allows prairie cooks to prepare this delicious seafood in a shell. Serve topped with a bit of fresh parsley.

Butter or margarine	2 tbsp.	30 mL
Finely chopped onion	1/3 cup	75 mL
Sliced fresh mushrooms	1 cup	250 mL
Garlic clove, minced	1	1
Butter or margarine	6 tbsp.	100 mL
All-purpose flour	6 tbsp.	100 mL
Salt	1/2 tsp.	2 mL
Pepper	1/8 tsp.	0.5 mL
Milk	1 3/4 cups	400 mL
White wine (or alcohol-free wine)	1/4 cup	60 mL
Dry bread crumbs	1/2 cup	125 mL
Grated Swiss cheese	1/2 cup	125 mL
Canned shrimp, broken or small, drained, rinsed and drained	2 × 4 oz.	2 × 113 g

Melt first amount of butter in frying pan. Add onion, mushrooms and garlic. Sauté until soft and lightly browned. Remove to bowl.

Melt second amount of butter in same pan. Mix in flour, salt and pepper. Stir in milk and wine until it boils and thickens.

Add bread crumbs and cheese. Stir until cheese melts. Add shrimp and mushroom mixture. Stir. Spoon into 8 greased ovenproof shells. At this point shells may be frozen and kept for days or refrigerated until later the same day or the next day. Bake in 350°F (180°C) oven for about 15 minutes. Allow about 25 minutes for frozen shells. Makes 8 small servings.

Keep up with little digs if you want to bury love.

■❖■ TOURTIÈRE QUÉBÉCOISE ■■■■■■

Thanks to the French Canadians for this great meat pie. It is so good you will want to freeze some to keep it on hand.

Lean ground beef	1 lb.	454 g
Ground pork	$1/2$ lb.	225 g
Finely chopped onion	1 cup	250 mL
Salt	1 tsp.	5 mL
Pepper	$1/4$ tsp.	1 mL
Garlic	$1/4$ tsp.	1 mL
Cinnamon	$3/4$ tsp.	4 mL
Cloves	$1/8$ tsp.	0.5 mL
Cooked potatoes, riced	1 cup	250 mL
Unbaked 9 inch (22 cm) pie shell Pastry for top crust	1	1

Combine first 8 ingredients in large pot. Bring to a boil, stirring often. Simmer uncovered until no pink remains in meat.

Potatoes should be smooth and free from lumps. Add to meat mixture. It should be moist and thick. Cool thoroughly.

Fill pastry shell with mixture. Dampen edges. Fit pastry over top. Press and crimp to seal. Cut slits in top. Bake in 350°F (180°C) oven until browned, about 45 minutes. Cuts into 8 small wedges. Double recipe to allow larger servings for 8 people.

Pictured on page 17.

■❖■ STRAWBERRY GREENS ■■■■■■

A natural for the western provinces of Canada. Strawberries grown here are red right through. Very good.

Medium head lettuce, cut or torn	1	1
Whole or sliced strawberries	2 cups	500 mL
Sliced celery	1 cup	250 mL
Green onions, sliced	4	4
DRESSING		
Cooking oil	$1/4$ cup	50 mL
Vinegar	$1/4$ cup	50 mL
Granulated sugar	$1/4$ cup	50 mL
Salt	$1/4$ tsp.	1 mL
Hot pepper sauce	$1/8$ tsp.	0.5 mL

(continued on next page)

Combine first 4 ingredients in bowl.

Dressing: Mix all 5 ingredients in small bowl. Pour over salad. Toss and serve. Serves 8.

SEAFOOD CASSEROLE ▪❖▪

A seafood combination at its best. Crumb topping.

Cod fillets, cooked and flaked	1 lb.	454 g
Canned crab or lobster, drained	5 oz.	142 g
Canned small shrimp, drained	2 × 4 oz.	2 × 113 g
Canned flaked tuna, drained	2 × 6½ oz.	2 × 184 g
Scallops fresh or frozen	½ lb.	225 g
Boiling water		
SAUCE		
Butter or margarine	¼ cup	60 mL
All-purpose flour	¼ cup	60 mL
Parsley flakes	1½ tsp.	7 mL
Salt	1 tsp.	5 mL
Pepper	¼ tsp.	1 mL
Cayenne pepper	⅛ tsp.	0.5 mL
Onion powder	½ tsp.	2 mL
Paprika	½ tsp.	2 mL
Milk	2¼ cups	500 mL
TOPPING		
Butter or margarine	3 tbsp.	50 mL
Dry bread crumbs	1 cup	250 mL

Combine first 4 ingredients in bowl. Set aside.

Cook scallops in boiling water for 5 minutes. Drain. Add to fish and seafood in bowl.

Sauce: Melt butter in small saucepan. Mix in flour, parsley, salt, pepper, cayenne pepper, onion powder and paprika. Add milk, stirring until it boils and thickens. Pour over fish and seafood in bowl. Stir lightly. Turn into 3 quart (4 L) casserole.

Topping: Melt butter in small saucepan. Add bread crumbs. Stir to coat. Sprinkle over casserole. Bake uncovered in 350°F (180°C) oven until bubbly-hot and browned, about 25 minutes. Serves 8.

LOBSTER AND SHRIMP MOLD

In the Atlantic provinces where fresh seafood is abundant it may be used in this recipe. However, many find it very convenient to make this from the shelf. A real treat.

Unflavored gelatin powder	$1/4$ oz.	7 g
Water	$1/2$ cup	125 mL
Condensed tomato soup	$1/2$ x 10 oz.	$1/2$ x 284 mL
Finely chopped celery	$1/2$ cup	125 mL
Finely chopped green pepper	1 tbsp.	15 mL
Onion powder	$1/2$ tsp.	2 mL
Canned broken shrimp, drained	4 oz.	113 g
Canned lobster, drained, chopped	5 oz.	142 g
Cream cheese, softened	8 oz.	250 g
Mayonnaise	$1/2$ cup	125 mL

Parsley for garnish
Carrot curls for garnish
Assorted crackers

Sprinkle gelatin powder over water in small saucepan. Let stand 5 minutes.

Add $1/2$ can tomato soup. Heat through.

Add next 5 ingredients. Stir. Remove from heat.

Beat cream cheese and mayonnaise together in small bowl until smooth. Add to saucepan. Beat well. Pour into 4 cup (900 mL) fish mold. Chill.

Unmold. Garnish with parsley and carrot curls. Serve with assorted crackers. Serves 8.

You buy ducks and a cow when you want milk and quackers.

A real feast. This different, scrumptious stuffing may be doubled to ensure enough for everyone. Just wrap excess stuffing in foil and place beside fish to cook.

Salmon, head and tail removed, dressed	5 lbs.	2.25 kg
Lemon juice		
SALMON STUFFING		
Dry bread crumbs	3 cups	700 mL
Dry onion flakes	2 tbsp.	30 mL
Parsley flakes	1 tsp.	5 mL
Poultry seasoning	$1/2$ tsp.	2 mL
Salt	$1/2$ tsp.	2 mL
Pepper	$1/8$ tsp.	0.5 mL
Basil	$1/4$ tsp.	1 mL
Chopped unpeeled zucchini	$2/3$ cup	150 mL
Medium tomato, chopped	1	1
Butter or margarine, melted	$1/2$ cup	125 mL

Sprinkle cavity of salmon with lemon juice.

Salmon Stuffing: In medium bowl combine remaining 10 ingredients in order given. Stuff fish. Use picks to hold together. Wrap in long piece of foil. Place on baking pan. Bake in 450°F (230°C) oven allowing 15 minutes per inch (2.5 cm) thickness measured at thickest part. Fish will flake easily with fork when done. Slip a fork under the skin. Lift it off gently a little at a time. Remove top half of meat in sections, pulling it away from bones. Remove bones from bottom half. Turn fish to remove remaining skin. Break apart to serve. Serves 8.

Pictured on page 17.

Most pigs can really act. There is a lot of ham in them.

▪◆▪ONION CASSEROLE

Onions baked in a sauce are excellent. Prepare ahead and bake when ready.

Onions, thickly sliced	2 lbs.	1 kg
Cold water to cover		
Butter or margarine	¼ cup	60 mL
Milk	¾ cup	175 mL
Salt	2 tsp.	10 mL
Pepper	¼ tsp.	1 mL
Sour cream	⅓ cup	75 mL
Egg	1	1
Grated medium Cheddar cheese	½ cup	125 mL
TOPPING		
Butter or margarine	2 tbsp.	30 mL
Dry bread crumbs	½ cup	125 mL
Grated medium Cheddar cheese	½ cup	125 mL

Soak onion in cold water for 30 minutes. Drain.

Add butter, milk, salt and pepper to onion in saucepan. Bring to a boil. Simmer covered until tender, about 10 minutes. Pour into 2 quart (2.5 L) casserole.

Beat sour cream, egg and cheese together with a spoon. Pour over onion mixture.

Topping: Melt butter in small saucepan over medium heat. Stir in crumbs and cheese. Spread over casserole. Bake in 350°F (180°C) oven until hot and browned, about 25 minutes. Serves 8.

Note: If cooking onion casserole in the oven at the same time as baking potatoes, cook at onion temperature. Allow extra time for potatoes to cook.

▪◆▪ZUCCHINI PATTIES

A different way to serve this vegetable. Moist and good.

Eggs	3	3
Grated unpeeled zucchini	3 cups	750 mL
Grated Parmesan cheese	6 tbsp.	100 mL

(continued on next page)

All-purpose flour	$1/_2$ cup	125 mL
Baking powder	$3/_4$ tsp.	4 mL
Salt	$3/_4$ tsp.	4 mL
Pepper	$1/_8$ tsp.	0.5 mL
Onion powder	$3/_4$ tsp.	4 mL
Fine dry bread crumbs	6 tbsp.	100 mL
Butter or margarine	2 tbsp.	30 mL

Beat eggs in mixing bowl until frothy. Add next 8 ingredients, mixing well. Make patty type rounds using about 2 tbsp. (30 mL) zucchini mixture for each patty.

Melt butter in frying pan. Cook patties browning both sides about 2 minutes per side. Add more butter if needed. Makes 16 patties.

PACIFIC RICE

A terrific combination.

Long grain rice	3 cups	750 mL
Water	6 cups	1.5 L
Salt	$1 1/_2$ tsp.	7 mL
Butter or margarine	$1/_4$ cup	50 mL
Chopped onion	$3/_4$ cup	175 mL
Chopped celery	$1/_2$ cup	125 mL
Chopped green pepper	$1/_2$ cup	125 mL
Canned mushroom pieces, drained	10 oz.	284 mL
Egg, beaten	1	1
Poultry seasoning	$1/_2$ tsp.	2 mL
Salt	$1/_2$ tsp.	2 mL
Celery seed	$1/_4$ tsp.	1 mL
Pepper	$1/_4$ tsp.	1 mL

Combine rice, water and first amount of salt in saucepan. Cover. Bring to a boil. Simmer until tender and water has been absorbed, about 15 minutes.

Melt butter in frying pan. Add onion, celery and green pepper. Sauté until soft.

Add mushrooms. Stir and sauté for about 1 minute.

Add remaining ingredients, mixing well. Stir into rice. Serves 8.

■✦■ MASHED POTATOES

These are mashed with a small amount of cheese. More cheese may be added if desired. Can be prepared ahead and cooked in the oven until hot and browned.

Large potatoes, peeled	**8**	**8**
Boiling water		
Hot milk	**¹/₂ cup**	**125 mL**
Butter or margarine	**2 tbsp.**	**30 mL**
Salt	**¹/₂ tsp.**	**2 mL**
Pepper	**¹/₈ tsp.**	**0.5 mL**
Grated medium Cheddar cheese	**¹/₂ cup**	**125 mL**

Cook potatoes in boiling water until tender and soft. Drain.

Mash until all potatoes are broken up. Add milk, butter, salt and pepper. Mash well. If you like potatoes quite creamy add more hot milk.

Stir in cheese. Potatoes may be served immediately or put into greased 3 quart (4 L) casserole. Cover and bake in 350°F (180°C) oven for 30 minutes. Remove cover. Bake an additional 15 minutes. Serves 8.

CREAMY POTATOES: Omit cheese. Taste for salt and pepper. Mash well and serve.

■✦■ Canada

1. Tourtière Québécoise page 10
2. Baked Salmon page 13
3. Maple Syrup Pie page 21

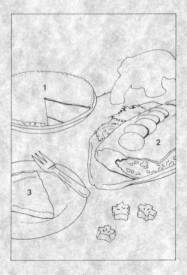

CARROT COINS ▪🍁▪

A very popular and colorful vegetable. Cooked in a sauce until tender.

Butter or margarine	¹/₄ cup	60 mL
Thinly sliced onion	1 cup	250 mL
All-purpose flour	2 tbsp.	30 mL
Salt	1 tsp.	5 mL
Pepper	¹/₈ tsp.	0.5 mL
Granulated sugar	1¹/₂ tsp.	7 mL
Water	1¹/₂ cups	375 mL
Thinly sliced carrots	8 cups	2 L

Melt butter in large saucepan. Add onion. Sauté until soft and golden brown.

Mix in flour, salt, pepper and sugar. Stir in water until it boils and thickens.

Add carrots. Cover. Bring to a boil. Simmer slowly until tender about 20 minutes. Serves 8.

VINAIGRETTE SALAD ▪🍁▪

A tasty green mixture with red pimiento and yellow cheese added. To be authentic, French Canadian cooks would add more cooking oil. Do try this version.

Mixed salad greens, cut or torn, lightly packed	8 cups	2 L
Sliced celery	1 cup	250 mL
Chopped pimiento	2-3 tbsp.	30-45 mL
Grated medium Cheddar cheese	1 cup	250 mL
DRESSING		
Cooking oil	3 tbsp.	50 mL
Vinegar	3 tbsp.	50 mL
Granulated sugar	1 tbsp.	15 mL
Salt	¹/₄ tsp.	1 mL
Prepared mustard	1 tsp.	5 mL

Combine first 4 ingredients in large bowl. Mix together. Chill until shortly before needed.

Dressing: Measure all 5 ingredients into small bowl. Whisk to blend. Pour over salad at the last moment. Toss. Serves 8.

▪️🍁▪️RHUBARB CRISP

Serve warm with ice cream or cold with pouring cream. A spring treat as well as an all-year-round one if you have frozen rhubarb.

Rhubarb, red preferred, cut in 1/2 inch (12 mm) lengths	7 cups	1.6 L
Granulated sugar	1³/₄ cups	400 mL
All-purpose flour	2 tbsp.	30 mL
Brown sugar, packed	1 cup	250 mL
All-purpose flour	1/2 cup	125 mL
Quick cooking rolled oats	1/2 cup	125 mL
Salt	1/2 tsp.	2 mL
Butter or margarine, softened	1/2 cup	125 mL

Place rhubarb into 10 inch (25 cm) casserole.

Mix first amounts of sugar and flour together. Pour over rhubarb.

Combine remaining ingredients in bowl until butter is mixed in and mixture is crumbly. Spread over top of casserole. Pat down lightly. Bake uncovered in 375°F (190°C) oven for about 40 to 50 minutes until browned and rhubarb is cooked. Serves 8.

▪️🍁▪️SASKATOON PIE

Definitely a prairie pie. For those that have no access to saskatoons, blueberries may be substituted. Good served with ice cream, whipped cream or slices of medium Cheddar cheese.

Pastry for 2 crust pie

Saskatoons	4 cups	1 L
Granulated sugar	1 cup	250 mL
All-purpose flour	1/4 cup	50 mL
Salt	1/4 tsp.	1 mL
Cinnamon	1/4 tsp.	1 mL
Lemon juice	1¹/₂ tbsp.	25 mL

Granulated sugar, sprinkle

(continued on next page)

Roll pastry for bottom crust to fit 9 inch (22 cm) pie plate. Trim edge.

In large bowl mix next 5 ingredients. Turn into prepared pie crust.

Drizzle lemon juice over top. Roll top crust. Dampen edges of bottom crust. Place on pie. Trim pastry. Crimp edges. Cut slits in top.

Sprinkle with remaining sugar. Bake in 350°F (180°C) oven on bottom shelf until browned and fruit is cooked, about 45 to 55 minutes. This will divide into 8 small pieces. It is better to make 2 pies and cut each into 6 wedges.

BLUEBERRY PIE: Use blueberries instead of saskatoons.

MAPLE SYRUP PIE

A superb pie suited to the maple syrup region. Maple flavored syrup may be substituted for the sake of economy.

Eggs	2	2
Brown sugar, packed	1 cup	250 mL
All-purpose flour	2 tbsp.	30 mL
Butter or margarine, softened	3 tbsp.	50 mL
Maple syrup	1 cup	250 mL
Chopped walnuts	¾ cup	175 mL
Vanilla	1 tsp.	5 mL
Unbaked 9 inch (22 cm) pie shell	1	1

Beat eggs in mixing bowl until frothy. Add sugar, flour and butter. Beat until smooth.

Mix in syrup, walnuts and vanilla.

Pour into pie shell. Bake in 375°F (190°C) oven until set, about 40 minutes.

Pictured on page 17.

China has opened its doors. Five thousand years of history is revealed at The Great Wall, Dragon Boat Festivals, splendid ice sculptures, and numerous religious and political monuments.

The world has not only adopted Chinese inventions such as paper and fireworks but has also taken to its popular cuisine.

Chinese cooking makes the most of everything and food is prepared in the most efficient way. In Hong Kong, for instance, where ovens are scarce, stir-fry is the norm.

Chinese cuisine lends itself to informal dining. After the customary soup course, a variety of dishes are set in the center of the table and everyone helps themselves. Green or black tea is served throughout the meal (never with cream or sugar). If you use chopsticks, it's a good idea to cut food into bite size pieces. Rice is cooked until sticky rather than fluffy, making it easier to eat with chopsticks. Salt is never added to rice. Dessert is not expected, although fortune cookies are popular in North America. In China, fresh fruit is often served to finish the meal.

May your table be honored with many guests as you enjoy this popular fare!

MENU 1

*Pork Ball Soup   Page 28
Pot Stickers   Page 26 *or*
*Spring Rolls   Page 24
*Plum Sauce   Page 25
Peppered Beef   Page 30
Stir-Fried Shrimp   Page 29
Red Tenderloin   Page 40
Almond Chicken   Page 39
Fried Rice   Page 32
*Broccoli And Carrots   Page 33
Tea

MENU 2

Egg Flower Soup   Page 27
*Shrimp Balls   Page 23
Slivered Beef   Page 31
Scallops In Oyster Sauce   Page 28
*Spare Ribs   Page 37
*Chicken Pepper   Page 38
*Rice With Pimiento   Page 34 *or*
Basic Rice   Page 32
Greens   Page 37
Tea

*Pictured page 35

These little balls look so attractive on a plate. Good choice for an appetizer. They freeze well.

Large shrimp or prawns, shelled and deveined, ground or finely minced	1 lb.	454 g
Egg whites	2	2
Soy sauce	2 tsp.	10 mL
Cornstarch	2 tsp.	10 mL
Salt	$\frac{1}{2}$ tsp.	2 mL
Ginger	$\frac{1}{4}$ tsp.	1 mL
Fine dry bread crumbs	$\frac{1}{2}$ cup	125 mL

Fat for deep-frying

Seafood sauce, ketchup or lemon juice

Mix first 7 ingredients together. Shape into $\frac{3}{4}$ inch (2 cm) balls. You should get 48 balls.

Deep-fry in hot 375°F (190°C) fat until browned. Drain on paper towels.

Serve with seafood sauce, ketchup or lemon juice for dipping. May be placed directly on plate or put 3 balls on small wooden skewer. Serve 2 skewers per plate. Serves 8 people 6 shrimp balls each.

He has a two story house. It was one story before he bought it and quite another story after.

SPRING ROLLS

These egg rolls are one of the best ways to start a meal.

Cooking oil	2 tbsp.	30 mL
Medium pork chop	1	1
Chopped onion	1/3 cup	75 mL
Shredded bok choy or cabbage, packed	1 cup	250 mL
Chopped fresh mushrooms	1 cup	250 mL
Fresh bean sprouts	1 cup	250 mL
Cooked chopped shrimp, fresh or canned	1/2 cup	125 mL
Bamboo shoots, shredded	1/2 cup	125 mL
Soy sauce	2 tsp.	10 mL
Parsley flakes	1/2 tsp.	2 mL
Granulated sugar	1/2 tsp.	2 mL
Salt	1/2 tsp.	2 mL
Pepper	1/8 tsp.	0.5 mL
Egg roll wrappers, about 5 inches (13 cm) square, see Note	1 lb.	454 mL
Fat for deep-frying		

Heat cooking oil in frying pan. Remove fat from pork chop. Cut meat into strips about 1 inch (2.5 cm) wide. Then cut into very thin pieces to look like short pieces of string. Add to hot fat. Add onion. Stir-fry until no pink remains in meat and onions are soft, about 3 minutes.

Add cabbage and mushrooms. Stir-fry until soft, about 2 minutes.

Add bean sprouts. Stir-fry for 2 minutes.

Add next 7 ingredients. Stir to mix well. Remove from heat. Cool. Divide mixture in half, then in half again. Continue until you have 16 piles of equal amounts. Cool.

Place 1 pile cooled mixture between the center and a corner of egg roll wrapper. Fold corner over filling. Fold both side corners over, tucking in as you turn. Roll over away from you. Wrap snugly. Moisten edges with water to seal.

(continued on next page)

Cook in deep-fryer in 375°F (190°C) fat, seam side down, turning once until browned, about 2½ to 3 minutes total time. Drain on paper towels. Serve hot with Plum Sauce, below. Serves 8 people 2 per plate.

Note: To eat with chopsticks, cut rolls diagonally into 1 to 1½ inch (2.5 to 3.5 cm) strips before placing on plate. Keep warm in 275°F (140°C) oven until serving time. To serve 1 egg roll each buy the larger eggroll wrappers, about 8 inches (20 cm) square. Divide filling into 8 piles only.

Pictured on page 35.

PLUM SAUCE

Very tasty over egg rolls.

Strained plums (baby food)	2 × 4½ oz.	2 × 128 mL
Cider vinegar	2 tbsp.	30 mL
Granulated sugar	2 tsp.	10 mL

Combine strained plums, vinegar and sugar in small saucepan. Heat and stir to dissolve sugar. Cool. Use as a dip for spring rolls. Makes 1 cup (225 mL).

Pictured on page 35.

Paré Pointer

It's a mystery who came off the ark first. It is written that Noah came forth.

POT STICKERS

These are so good you may have to limit how many you serve to ensure there are still appetites for the next course.

Ground pork	1 lb.	454 g
Canned broken shrimp, drained	4 oz.	113 g
Suey choy, ground and drained	1 cup	250 mL
Dry onion flakes	1 tbsp.	15 mL
Soy sauce	1 tbsp.	15 mL
Salt	1 tsp.	5 mL
Ginger	1/2 tsp.	2 mL
Garlic powder	1/4 tsp.	1 mL
Wonton or egg roll wrappers	1 lb.	454 g
Boiling water	4 qts.	5 L
Margarine or cooking oil	2 tbsp.	30 mL

Combine first 8 ingredients in bowl. Mix well.

Cut wrappers into $2^3/_4$ inch (7 cm) circles. Put 1 tsp. (5 mL) filling in center. Dampen edges with water. Fold over. Press to seal.

Boil water in large uncovered pot. Drop some dumplings into boiling water. Boil and cook for about 5 minutes. Allow full 5 minutes to ensure that pork is cooked. Use slotted spoon to remove to plate. These may be prepared ahead, chilled, then browned when needed.

Heat margarine in frying pan. Arrange dumplings close together. Fry on 1 side only until quite brown. Serve brown side up with Hot Savory Sauce for dipping. Makes about 55 to 60. Serves 8 with a few leftover to freeze or eat next day.

HOT SAVORY SAUCE

Tomato sauce	$7^1/_2$ oz.	213 mL
Soy sauce	2 tbsp.	30 mL
Vinegar	1 tbsp.	15 mL
Ginger	1/4 tsp.	1 mL
Garlic powder	1/4 tsp.	1 mL
Salt	1/4 tsp.	1 mL
Cayenne pepper	1/4 tsp.	1 mL

Combine all ingredients in small saucepan over medium heat. Bring to a boil. Simmer for about 1 minute so flavors blend. Makes about 3/4 cup (175 mL) spicy-hot dip.

A soft looking soup. Not too filling before a meal.

Chicken bouillon cubes	6	6
Boiling water	9 cups	2 L
Eggs, beaten	3	3
Cornstarch	$1/_3$ cup	75 mL
Water	$1/_3$ cup	75 mL
Salt	$1/_2$ tsp.	2 mL
Pepper	$1/_8$ tsp.	0.5 mL
Soy sauce	1 tbsp.	15 mL
Thinly sliced green onion	1 tbsp.	15 mL

Dissolve bouillon cubes in boiling water in Dutch oven.

Pour eggs slowly into boiling broth stirring continually until eggs are cooked.

Mix next 5 ingredients together in small bowl. Stir into boiling broth until it returns to a boil and thickens. Ladle soup into 8 bowls.

Top each bowl with a few slices of onion. Serves 8 people about 1 cup (250 mL) each.

Paré Pointer

When you've seen a water cooler you've seen a thirst aid kit.

◀ ▩ ▶ PORK BALL SOUP ━━━━━━━━━━

Delicious meatballs surrounded by broth and greens.

Boiling water	9 cups	2 L
Chicken bouillon cubes, crumbled	7 x ⅕ oz.	7 x 6 g
Ground pork	1 lb.	454 g
Soy sauce	1 tbsp.	15 mL
All-purpose flour	2 tsp.	10 mL
Salt	¾ tsp.	4 mL
Chinese spinach, cut up, packed (or use bok choy or suey choy)	1½ cups	375 mL
Oyster sauce	2 tbsp.	30 mL

Measure water into large saucepan. Bring to a boil over medium heat. Dissolve bouillon cubes in boiling water.

In medium bowl mix pork with soy sauce. Sprinkle with flour and salt. Mix well. Shape into small balls about ¾ inch (2 cm) diameter. You should have 80 balls. Drop into boiling water. Cover. Boil 15 minutes.

Add spinach and oyster sauce. Boil for 5 minutes more. Serves 8 people about 1 cup (225 mL) each.

Pictured on page 35.

◀ ▩ ▶ SCALLOPS IN OYSTER SAUCE ━━━━━━

Snow peas add color to this delicious dish.

Cooking oil	2 tbsp.	30 mL
Thinly sliced onion	1 cup	250 mL
Large scallops, halved	1½ lbs.	700 g
Bamboo shoots, sliced in sticks	10 oz.	284 mL
Snow peas	10 oz.	284 g
Oyster sauce	2 tbsp.	30 mL
Ketchup	1 tbsp.	15 mL
Soy sauce	1 tsp.	5 mL
Granulated sugar	½ tsp.	2 mL
Salt	½ tsp.	2 mL
Water	¼ cup	60 mL
Cornstarch	1 tbsp.	15 mL
Chicken bouillon powder	1 tsp.	5 mL

(continued on next page)

Heat cooking oil in wok or frying pan. Add onion. Fry until soft.

Add scallops and bamboo shoots. Stir-fry to partially cook scallops, about 3 minutes.

After scallops have partially cooked add snow peas. If you are using the frozen ones, thaw completely under cold running water. Add to wok. Stir-fry for about 2 minutes more.

Stir remaining ingredients together in small bowl. Pour over scallop mixture. Stir until thickened. Serves 8.

STIR-FRIED SHRIMP

This is very quick to prepare once the shrimp is ready. The addition of green peas adds color and flavor.

Cooking oil	3 tbsp.	50 mL
Medium shrimp, shelled and deveined	40-48	40-48
Vinegar	1/4 cup	60 mL
Brown sugar, packed	1/4 cup	60 mL
Ketchup	2 tbsp.	30 mL
Water	1/4 cup	60 mL
Ginger	1/4 tsp.	1 mL
Garlic powder	1/4 tsp.	1 mL
Onion powder	1/4 tsp.	1 mL
Salt	1/4 tsp.	1 mL
Cornstarch	1 tbsp.	15 mL
Frozen peas	10 oz.	284 g

Heat cooking oil in wok or frying pan. Add shrimp. Cook, stirring often until they curl and turn pinkish.

Combine next 9 ingredients in small bowl. Stir into shrimp until it thickens.

Run frozen peas under warm water to thaw. Add to wok. Stir-fry to cook, about 2 minutes. Serves 8.

Pictured on page 35.

PEPPERED BEEF

Don't be put off by the length of this recipe. It is easy to do. You can never tell it contains so much pepper.

Sirloin steak	2 lbs.	900 g
Unseasoned meat tenderizer		
White wine (or alcohol-free wine)	1 tbsp.	15 mL
Soy sauce	1 tbsp.	15 mL
Granulated sugar	1 tbsp.	15 mL
Cooking oil	1 tbsp.	15 mL
Pepper	2 tsp.	10 mL
Water	1½ cup	375 mL
Cooking oil	2 tbsp.	30 mL
Beef bouillon cubes, crumbled	3	3
Boiling water	2 cups	500 mL
Medium carrots, sliced	4	4
Chopped onion	1 cup	250 mL
Ginger	¼ tsp.	1 mL
Garlic powder	¼ tsp.	1 mL
Canned cut green beans, drained	14 oz.	398 mL
Cornstarch	1½ tbsp.	25 mL
Water	2 tbsp.	30 mL

Sprinkle steak with tenderizer. Poke holes all over. Turn and repeat on other side. Let stand 30 minutes. Cut into 1 inch (2.5 cm) cubes.

Combine next 6 ingredients in deep bowl. Add steak. Mix. Marinate for 20 minutes.

Heat second amount of cooking oil in frying pan. Take meat from marinade and brown in hot cooking oil.

Dissolve bouillon cubes in boiling water in large saucepan. Add beef. Cover. Bring to a boil. Simmer for 1 hour. There should be enough liquid if it is simmered slowly. Check once or twice and add a bit more if needed.

Add carrot, onion, ginger and garlic. Return to a simmer. Cook until meat and carrots are tender, about 30 minutes.

Add green beans. Heat through.

Mix cornstarch in remaining water. Pour into meat mixture. Stir until it boils and thickens. Serves 8.

Tender tasty strips of beef with baby corn and some sliced carrots.

All-purpose flour	$^1/_2$ **cup**	125 mL
Salt	$^1/_2$ **tsp.**	2 mL
Pepper	$^1/_8$ **tsp.**	0.5 mL
Sirloin steak, cut in thin short strips	**2 lbs.**	900 g
Cooking oil	$^1/_4$ **cup**	50 mL
Thinly sliced celery	$^1/_2$ **cup**	125 mL
Grated carrot	**1 cup**	250 mL
Thinly sliced onion	**1 cup**	250 mL
Green pepper, thinly sliced	**1**	1
Canned baby corn cobs, drained	**14 oz.**	398 mL
SAUCE		
Beef bouillon powder	**1 tsp.**	5 mL
Cornstarch	**1 tbsp.**	15 mL
Water	$^1/_4$ **cup**	50 mL
Soy sauce	**2 tbsp.**	30 mL
Ketchup	**2 tbsp.**	30 mL
Garlic powder	$^1/_4$ **tsp.**	1 mL

Combine flour, salt and pepper in bag. Add meat pieces. Shake to coat.

Heat cooking oil in wok or frying pan. Add meat. Stir-fry for about 10 minutes. Remove meat to bowl.

Combine celery, carrot, onion and green pepper in wok or frying pan. Add more cooking oil if needed. Stir-fry until soft, about 5 minutes.

Stir in corn. Add meat.

Sauce: Mix bouillon powder, cornstarch and water together in small bowl.

Add remaining sauce ingredients. Stir. Pour over vegetables and beef. Stir until thickened and meat is coated. Serves 8.

◣■FRIED RICE

Very easy. A beaten egg mixture is stirred into hot rice.

Cooking oil	2 tbsp.	30 mL
Leftover cooked cold rice, separated with wet hands	8 cups	1.8 L
Eggs, beaten	4	4
Soy sauce	2 tbsp.	30 mL
Green onions, sliced	4-6	4-6
Water	$^1/_4$ cup	50 mL
Granulated sugar	1 tsp.	5 mL
Salt	$^1/_2$ tsp.	2 mL

Heat cooking oil in wok. Add rice. Stir until piping hot.

In small bowl combine remaining ingredients. Stir. Pour all at once over rice. Stir until egg is cooked, about 3 minutes. Serves 8.

SEAFOOD FRIED RICE: Add 2 cups (500 mL) chopped cooked shrimp or crab.

MEATY FRIED RICE: Add 2 cups (500 mL) cooked slivered pork or beef.

VEGETABLE FRIED RICE: Add 2 cups (500 mL) cooked vegetables in small pieces.

CHICKEN FRIED RICE: Add 2 cups (500 mL) cooked slivered chicken.

◣■BASIC RICE

A standard dish in every household.

Long grain rice	3 cups	700 mL
Water	$4^1/_2$ cups	1 L

Wash rice two or three times. Combine rice with water in heavy saucepan. Bring to a boil uncovered. Turn heat down. Cover. Simmer until all liquid has been absorbed. Fluff with fork. If too moist, continue to cook until dried to proper texture.

Serves 8.

When button mushrooms are added this is quite elegant.

Broccoli florets and thinly sliced peeled stems	**4 cups**	**1 L**
Boiling salted water		
Cooking oil	**1 tbsp.**	**15 mL**
Chicken bouillon cubes, crumbled	**2 x $^1/_5$ oz.**	**2×6 g**
Boiling water	**1$^1/_2$ cups**	**375 mL**
Thinly sliced carrots	**1$^1/_2$ cups**	**375 mL**
Canned button mushrooms, drained	**10 oz.**	**284 mL**
Salt	**$^3/_4$ tsp.**	**4 mL**
Granulated sugar	**$^1/_2$ tsp.**	**2 mL**
Soy sauce	**1 tsp.**	**5 mL**
Cornstarch	**1 tbsp.**	**15 mL**
Water	**4 tsp.**	**20 mL**

Cook broccoli in boiling salted water for 2 minutes. Drain. Rinse in cold water and drain well.

Heat cooking oil in wok or frying pan. Add broccoli. Sauté over high heat quickly, about 2 minutes. Turn into bowl.

Dissolve chicken cubes in second amount of boiling water. Add to wok.

Add carrots. Simmer until tender, about 8 minutes. Add broccoli.

Add mushrooms, salt, sugar and soy sauce. Stir-fry until hot.

Mix cornstarch in remaining water. Stir into vegetables until thickened. Serves 8.

Pictured on page 35.

They called their little pig "Ink" because he always ran out of the pen.

RICE WITH PIMIENTO

Colorful and so very good. Contains no salt.

Long grain rice	2 cups	500 mL
Boiling water	4 cups	1 L
Canned chopped pimiento	1 tbsp.	15 mL
Butter or margarine	2 tbsp.	30 mL
Green onions, sliced	2	2
Soy sauce	4 tsp.	20 mL
Granulated sugar	1/2 tsp.	2 mL

Rinse rice in cold water until it runs clear. Drain. Cook rice in boiling water until water is absorbed and rice is tender, about 15 minutes.

Add remaining ingredients. Stir to mix well. Serves 8.

Pictured on page 35.

China

Looks like a mixed garden of greens.

Cooking oil	2 tbsp.	30 mL
Bok choy or suey choy, cut in short narrow strips	3 cups	750 mL
Fresh bean sprouts, large handful	1	1
Snow peas, frozen or fresh	10 oz.	284 g
Spinach or lettuce, cut up, lightly packed	1$\frac{1}{2}$ cups	375 mL
Chicken bouillon powder	1 tsp.	5 mL
Boiling water	$\frac{1}{2}$ cup	125 mL
Salt	$\frac{1}{2}$ tsp.	2 mL
Granulated sugar	$\frac{1}{2}$ tsp.	2 mL

Heat cooking oil in wok or frying pan. Add bok choy, bean sprouts, snow peas and spinach. Stir-fry until limp, about 3 minutes.

Mix bouillon powder with boiling water in cup. Add salt and sugar. Pour over vegetables. Stir. Cover and cook for about 2 minutes. Serves 8.

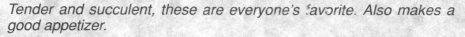

Tender and succulent, these are everyone's favorite. Also makes a good appetizer.

Vinegar	$\frac{1}{2}$ cup	125 mL
Honey or syrup	$\frac{1}{4}$ cup	60 mL
Granulated sugar	$\frac{1}{4}$ cup	60 mL
Soy sauce	$\frac{1}{2}$ cup	125 mL
Garlic powder	$\frac{1}{2}$ tsp.	2 mL
Ginger	$\frac{1}{2}$ tsp.	2 mL
Water	2 cups	500 mL
Chicken bouillon powder	4 tsp.	20 mL
Spareribs, cut in 1$\frac{1}{2}$ (4 cm) lengths	6 lbs.	2.7 kg

Combine first 8 ingredients in deep bowl. Stir well.

Add ribs. Stir to coat all ribs. Cover. Chill overnight. Stir occasionally. Transfer ribs to roaster. Reserve marinade. Cover roaster. Cook in 350°F (180°C) oven for about 1 hour until tender. Baste with marinade 2 or 3 times during cooking. To brown, remove lid and run under broiler for a few minutes. Serves 8.

Pictured on page 35.

CHICKEN PEPPER

Colorful and delicious.

Chicken thighs	6	6
Chicken breasts	2	2
Water	1 cup	250 mL
Soy sauce	1/4 cup	60 mL
Cornstarch	2 tbsp.	30 mL
Salt	1 tsp.	5 mL
Pepper	1/4 tsp.	1 mL
Cooking oil	3 tbsp.	50 mL
Large onion, cut bite size	1	1
Red peppers or mixture of red, green and yellow, cut bite size	4	4
Water	1 cup	250 mL
Chicken bouillon powder	2 tsp.	10 mL
Sherry	1 tbsp.	15 mL
Soy sauce	1 tbsp.	15 mL
Cornstarch	4 tsp.	20 mL

Cut meat from thighs and breasts. Cut into bite size pieces.

Mix next 5 ingredients together in deep bowl. Add chicken. Let marinate for 15 minutes.

Heat cooking oil in wok or frying pan. Put chicken into wok. Stir-fry in hot oil until cooked. Remove chicken to bowl.

Put onion into wok. Stir-fry until soft.

Add peppers. Cook until tender. Add chicken. Heat through.

Mix remaining ingredients together in small bowl. Pour over all. Stir-fry until thickened. Turn out onto warm platter or bowl. Serves 8.

One of the most popular dishes.

Cooking oil	3 tbsp.	50 mL
Chicken breasts, skin removed, boned, cut bite size	3	3
Salt	1 tsp.	5 mL
Sliced celery	1 cup	250 mL
Fresh mushrooms, sliced	2 cups	500 mL
Frozen snow peas, thawed	10 oz.	284 g
Green onions, sliced	4	4
Salt	1/2 tsp.	2 mL
Cornstarch	1 tbsp.	15 mL
Granulated sugar	1 tsp.	5 mL
Chicken bouillon powder	1 tsp.	5 mL
Cold water	1/2 cup	125 mL
Almonds, slivered or sliced, toasted in 350° F (180° C) oven until browned, stirring twice	1 cup	250 mL

Heat cooking oil in wok or large frying pan. Add chicken and first amount of salt. Stir-fry until cooked, about 10 minutes. Transfer to bowl.

If no cooking oil is left in wok, add 1 tbsp. (15 mL). Add celery. Stir-fry for 4 minutes.

Add mushrooms. Stir-fry for 3 minutes.

Add snow peas, green onion and second amount of salt. Stir-fry for 2 minutes.

Stir cornstarch, sugar and bouillon powder into water. Pour into wok. Stir-fry to cook and thicken. Add chicken. Stir until heated through. Turn into warm shallow bowl.

Sprinkle with almonds. Serves 8.

Dark crusted and very good. A super choice for a meat dish.

Soy sauce	¹/₄ cup	60 mL
Granulated sugar	2 tbsp.	30 mL
Salt	2 tsp.	10 mL
Cinnamon	¹/₄ tsp.	1 mL
Cloves	¹/₄ tsp.	1 mL
Aniseed	¹/₄ tsp.	1 mL
Thyme	¹/₄ tsp.	1 mL
Garlic powder	¹/₄ tsp.	1 mL
Ginger	¹/₄ tsp.	1 mL
Pork tenderloins, about 2 lbs. (900 g)	4	4

Mix first 9 ingredients together in small bowl.

Brush sauce over meat. Let stand for 30 minutes. Put into roaster. Roast uncovered in 425°F (220°C) oven for 15 minutes. Turn oven down to 350°F (180°C). Cover. Cook for about 30 minutes more. Slice thinly in diagonal slices. Arrange on warm plate. Serves 8.

The main difference between dinosaurs and dragons is that dinosaurs are too young to smoke.

FRANCE

France, with its brisk modern cities and sleepy country villages boasts of being the world's most civilized society. People from all over the world meet here to enjoy Mediterranean beaches, the Louvre, quiet and not-so-quiet sidewalk cafés and, of course, superb food and wine.

The art of good eating and cooking is greatly appreciated by the French. Specialty food shops and cafés line streets everywhere. A great deal of care and attention is paid to food preparation. And the food is enjoyed with some of the best, if not **the** best, wine in the world. As would be expected, regional cuisine varies and is usually accompanied by wine produced in the area.

French dining is considered to be the most sophisticated anywhere. However, in your home, you may want to be less formal. Be sure to serve a long narrow loaf of French bread (baquette) with your meal. An informal dinner may still consist of several courses; soup may be followed by salad, then meat (almost always served with sauce) vegetables and potatoes, and finally dessert . Often salad is served between the main course and dessert. Petits fours or chocolates and coffee round off the meal.

Bon appetit!

MENU 1

Crab Bisque Page 42
*Niçoise Salad Page 44
Steak Filet in Juice Page 49 *or*
*Chicken In Cherry Sauce Page 46
*Potato Croquettes Page 48
*Vegetable Tart Page 50
*Snow Eggs Page 55
Coffee

MENU 2

French Onion Soup Page 42
Shrimp Salad Page 44
Sole Veronique Page 47 *or*
Veal Cutlets in Wine Sauce Page 52
Crumbed Potatoes Page 45
Broccoli Patch Page 43
Strawberry Cream Cake Page 56
Coffee

*Pictured on cover

FRENCH ONION SOUP

One of the best food treats in France. You will need oven-proof bowls for this scrumptious soup.

Butter or margarine	6 tbsp.	100 mL
Onions, peeled, thinly sliced (about 7)	2½ lbs.	1.13 kg
Granulated sugar	1 tbsp.	15 mL
All-purpose flour	2 tbsp.	30 mL
Salt	½ tsp.	2 mL
Pepper	¼ tsp.	1 mL
Beef bouillon cubes	7 × ⅕ oz.	7 × 6 g
Boiling water	8 cups	1.8 L
French bread slices, toasted and cubed	8	8
Grated Gruyère cheese	2 cups	500 mL

Melt butter in frying pan. Add onion and sugar. Sauté slowly until medium brown in color, stirring often.

Sprinkle with flour, salt and pepper. Stir and cook for 5 minutes.

Dissolve bouillon cubes in boiling water in large saucepan. Add contents of frying pan. Bring to a boil. Simmer covered for 20 minutes.

Cover bottom of 8 bowls with toast cubes. Divide soup over top. Place about ¼ cup (50 mL) cheese over soup. Broil to melt and brown cheese. Serves 8.

CRAB BISQUE

Blender smooth. Just the right thickness. Just the right flavor.

Butter or margarine	3 tbsp.	50 mL
Finely chopped onion	2 cups	500 mL
Garlic clove, minced	1	1
Chicken bouillon cubes	6 × ⅕ oz.	6 × 6 g
Boiling water	1 cup	250 mL

(continued on next page)

Water	3½ cups	800 mL
Tomato sauce	2 tbsp.	30 mL
Long grain rice	⅓ cup	75 mL
Crabmeat, fresh or canned, cartilage removed	2 cups	450 mL
Salt	½ tsp.	2 mL
Pepper	⅛ tsp.	0.5 mL
Cayenne pepper, just a pinch		
Saffron or turmeric, just a pinch		
Milk	2 cups	450 mL
White wine (or alcohol-free wine)	1 cup	225 mL

Melt butter in large saucepan. Add onion and garlic. Sauté until soft but not browned.

Dissolve bouillon cubes in boiling water in small container. Add to onions.

Stir in next 9 ingredients. Bring to a boil. Simmer covered until rice is tender, about 15 minutes. Cool a bit. Run through blender. Strain through sieve. Return to saucepan.

Add wine. Return to a boil. Remove from heat and serve with a few croutons on top or on the side. Serves 8 people 1 cup (225 mL) each.

CROUTONS

Butter or margarine	2 tbsp.	30 mL
Cooking oil	2 tbsp.	30 mL
White bread slices, firm or partially dry, crusts removed, diced	5	5

Heat butter and cooking oil in frying pan.

Add diced bread. Fry until browned. Stir often, turning cubes as much as possible. Remove and cool.

SHRIMP SALAD

Fruit wedges are topped with a yummy shrimp sauce.

Small head of lettuce, shredded	1	1
Thin slices of canteloupe or papaya	32	32
Thin slices of honeydew	24	24
TOPPING		
Mayonnaise	³/₄ cup	175 mL
Chili sauce	¹/₃ cup	75 mL
Sweet pickle relish	2 tbsp.	30 mL
Onion powder	¹/₄ tsp.	1 mL
Canned cocktail shrimp, rinsed and drained	2 × 4 oz.	2 × 113 g

Divide and spread lettuce over 8 salad plates. Halve and seed melons. Slice and peel. Overlap 4 slices canteloupe and 3 slices honeydew on each plate beginning and ending with canteloupe.

Topping: Combine first 4 ingredients in bowl. Stir.

Carefully fold in shrimp. Spoon across melon. Serves 8.

NIÇOISE SALAD

A NEES-swahs salad contains everything you need for a complete meal in small quantities.

Medium potatoes, peeled	4	4
Boiling salted water		
Canned cut green beans, drained	14 oz.	398 mL
Finely chopped onion	¹/₂ cup	125 mL
DRESSING		
Cooking oil	¹/₂ cup	125 mL
Red wine vinegar	¹/₄ cup	60 mL
Salt	¹/₄ tsp.	1 mL
Pepper	¹/₈ tsp.	0.5 mL
Garlic powder	¹/₄ tsp.	1 mL
Prepared mustard	¹/₂ tsp.	2 mL
Chopped pimiento	2 oz.	57 mL

(continued on next page)

Tomatoes, peeled and cubed	3	3
Romaine lettuce	1	1
Black pitted olives	16-24	16-24
Green pimiento-stuffed olives	16-24	16-24
Hard-boiled eggs, quartered lengthwise	4	4
Canned tuna, drained, broken up	2 × 6 /₂ oz.	2 × 184 g

Cook potatoes in boiling salted water until tender. Drain. When cool enough to handle, dice into medium size pieces into large bowl.

Add green beans and onion.

Dressing: Combine first 7 Dressing ingredients in small bowl. Mix well. Pour over potato mixture. Toss to coat.

Dip tomatoes in boiling water until they peel easily, about 1 minute. Peel and cube. Line small salad plates or large plate with lettuce leaves. Place potato mixture on top. Arrange tomatoes, olives, eggs and tuna over and around potato mixture. Serves 8.

Pictured on cover.

CRUMBED POTATOES

Simple but effective.

Medium potatoes, peeled and quartered	8	8
Boiling salted water		
Butter or margarine, melted	¹/₄ cup	60 mL
Dry bread crumbs	3 tbsp.	50 mL
Salt	¹/₄ tsp.	1 mL
Pepper, sprinkle		

Cook potatoes in boiling salted water until tender. Use tip of sharp knife to test rather than a fork. Drain. Return to heat to dry any remaining liquid. Watch closely.

Mix remaining ingredients together. Add to potatoes. Shake saucepan or toss to coat. Serves 8.

CHICKEN IN CHERRY SAUCE

This chicken is served with a savory sauce using canned cherries.

Margarine (butter browns too fast)	3 tbsp.	50 mL
Large chicken breasts, halved	4	4
Salt, sprinkle		
Pepper, sprinkle		

CHERRY SAUCE

Butter or margarine	3 tbsp.	50 mL
Chopped onion	1 cup	250 mL
Garlic clove, minced	1	1
Chopped celery	1/2 cup	125 mL
Grated carrot	1 cup	250 mL
All-purpose flour	1/4 cup	60 mL
Salt	1 tsp.	5 mL
Pepper	1/4 tsp.	1 mL
Cloves, just a pinch		
Beef bouillon powder	2 tsp.	10 mL
Water	1 cup	250 mL
Red wine	1/4 cup	60 mL
Canned cherries with juice, halve and discard pits	14 oz.	398 mL
Chopped walnuts	2-4 tbsp.	30-60 mL

Melt margarine in frying pan. Add chicken breasts. Brown well. Sprinkle with salt and pepper. Cover and cook until tender. Remove to another container to keep hot.

Cherry Sauce: Melt butter in frying pan. Add onion, garlic, celery and carrot. Sauté until soft.

Mix in flour, salt, pepper, cloves and bouillon powder. Add water and wine. Stir until it boils and thickens. Add pitted cherries and juice. Return to a boil.

Remove skin from chicken breast. Pull meat from bone keeping in one piece. To serve, chicken breast may be left in 1 piece or cut into slices. Lay slices, overlapping, on 1 side of plate. Spoon sauce over top.

Sprinkle with walnuts. Serve remainder of sauce in separate bowl. Makes 8 servings.

Pictured on cover.

These fish fillets are cooked, then for good measure, topped with a sauce containing grapes.

Sole fillets	3 lbs.	1.36 kg
Water	5 cups	1.12 L
White wine (or alcohol-free wine)	1 cup	225 mL
Salt	1 tsp.	5 mL
Pepper	1/4 tsp.	1 mL
Onion powder	1/2 tsp.	2 mL
Parsley flakes	2 tsp.	10 mL
SAUCE		
Butter or margarine	1/4 cup	60 mL
All-purpose flour	1/4 cup	60 mL
Salt	1/2 tsp.	2 mL
Pepper	1/8 tsp.	0.5 mL
Nutmeg, just a pinch		
Reserved fish stock	2 cups	450 mL
Whipping cream		
Seedless green grapes	1/2 lb.	225 g

Fold ends of fillets under. Arrange in greased Dutch oven. If fillets have skin, place skin-side down.

Measure next 6 ingredients into large saucepan. Stir. Bring to a boil, stirring occasionally. Pour over fish fillets. Bring to a boil. Cover. Simmer and poach for about 6 minutes until fish flakes easily when tested with fork. Carefully lift fish onto warm platter and keep hot. Strain liquid and reserve 2 cups (450 mL).

Sauce: Melt butter in frying pan. Mix in flour, salt, pepper and nutmeg. Stir in reserved fish stock until it boils and thickens. Add cream.

Remove from heat. Add grapes. Stir well. Do not boil or grapes will split open. Spoon over sole fillets. Serves 8.

◀▐▌▪POTATO CROQUETTES ━━━━━━━━━━

These browned crispy potatoes add much to the appearance of a meal.

Potatoes, peeled and cut	3 lbs.	1.36 kg
Boiling salted water		
Butter or margarine	6 tbsp.	100 mL
Salt	3/4 tsp.	4 mL
Pepper	1/4 tsp.	1 mL
Onion powder	1/8 tsp.	0.5 mL
Egg, fork beaten	1	1
All-purpose flour	1/4 cup	50 mL
Eggs, lightly beaten	2	2
Dry fine bread crumbs	1 cup	250 mL
Fat for deep-frying		

Cook potatoes in boiling salted water until fork tender. Drain. Allow potatoes to dry in pan over heat. Put through ricer or mash.

Add butter, salt, pepper, onion powder and first egg. Beat or mash well. Check seasoning and add more if desired. Shape into 3 inch (8 cm) cylinders of cigar thickness or balls the size of golf balls.

Coat cylinders with flour. Dip in second amount of beaten eggs then roll in bread crumbs.

Deep-fry in hot fat 375°F (180°C) until well-browned. As they are done, arrange in single layer on paper towel-lined tray. Keep hot in 300°F (150°C) oven. Serves 8.

Pictured on cover.

◀▐▌▪BROCCOLI PATCH ━━━━━━━━━━

A plateful of green tufts makes a good conversation piece.

Broccoli	3 lbs.	1.35 kg
Boiling water		
Butter or margarine	1/2 cup	125 mL
Seasoned salt	1 1/2 tsp.	7 mL

Cut broccoli, leaving stems about the same length as florets. Do not separate florets. Steam over boiling water until tender crisp. If you don't have a steamer, boil in water. Drain.

(continued on next page)

Melt butter in small saucepan. Stir in seasoned salt. Heat until light brown. Arrange circle of broccoli around outside edge of plate, placing stems toward center. Form a second, smaller circle, covering stems of first circle. Repeat until you have a big rounded puff. Rubber gloves help to speed this up. Drizzle butter over top. Serves 8.

STEAK FILET IN JUICE

Tender beef served with a sensational sauce.

French bread slices, cut to fit steaks	8	8
Cooking oil	1 tbsp.	15 mL
Butter or margarine	1 tbsp.	15 mL
Butter or margarine	2 tbsp.	30 mL
Thick beef tenderloin fillets	8	8
Salt, sprinkle		
Pepper, sprinkle		
SAUCE		
Water	1 cup	250 mL
Beef bouillon powder	2 tsp.	10 mL
Tomato sauce	2 tbsp.	30 mL
Red wine	1/4 cup	60 mL
Paprika	1 tbsp.	15 mL
Savory, scant measure	1/8 tsp.	0.5 mL
Onion salt	1/2 tsp.	2 mL
Garlic powder	1/8 tsp.	0.5 mL
Canned truffle slices (optional)	8	8

Sauté bread in cooking oil and first amount of butter. Brown both sides. Add more cooking oil and butter as needed. Remove to plate. Let stand at room temperature until needed.

Melt second amount of butter in same frying pan. Cook steaks to desired degree of doneness, browning both sides. Sprinkle with salt and pepper. Set on toast rounds. Keep warm in oven.

Sauce: Combine all 8 ingredients in same frying pan. Stir as you bring it to a boil. Loosen any bits left in pan.

Lay a slice of truffle on each steak. Spoon sauce over top. Serves 8.

VEGETABLE TART

A lengthy recipe but not difficult. Serving vegetables in a bread crust is different.

Loaf of frozen white bread dough, thawed	1	1

TOMATO SAUCE

Cooking oil	2 tbsp.	30 mL
Butter or margarine	1 tbsp.	15 mL
Chopped onion	1 cup	250 mL
Canned tomatoes	14 oz.	398 mL
Vegetable flakes	2 tsp.	10 mL
Salt	$1/2$ tsp.	2 mL
Pepper	$1/8$ tsp.	0.5 mL
Garlic powder (or 1 clove, minced)	$1/4$ tsp.	1 mL

VEGETABLES

Cooking oil	1 tbsp.	15 mL
Butter or margarine	1 tbsp.	15 mL
Eggplant ($1/2$ medium) cut matchstick size	$3^1/2$ cups	800 mL
Cooking oil	1 tbsp.	15 mL
Butter or margarine	1 tbsp.	15 mL
Medium zucchini, cut matchstick size	1	1

CREAM SAUCE

Butter or margarine	$1^1/2$ tbsp.	25 mL
All-purpose flour	$1^1/2$ tbsp.	25 mL
Salt	$1/2$ tsp.	2 mL
Pepper	$1/8$ tsp.	0.5 mL
Milk	$3/4$ cup	200 mL
Egg, fork beaten	1	1
Grated Gruyère cheese	$1/2$ cup	125 mL
Grated Gruyère cheese	$1/4$ cup	60 mL

(continued on next page)

Roll out bread dough to fit a 9 inch (22 cm) p e plate.

Tomato Sauce: Heat cooking oil and butter in frying pan. Add onion. Sauté until soft but not brown.

Add next 5 ingredients. Cook uncoverec until most liquid has evaporated, about 20 to 30 minutes. Stir often. Transfer to bowl.

Vegetables: Heat first amount of cooking oil and butter in same frying pan. Add eggplant. Sauté about 5 minutes until slightly softened. Stir often. Transfer to separate bowl.

Heat second amount of cooking oil and butter in same frying pan. Add zucchini. Sauté about 3 minutes until slightly softened. Stir often. Transfer to separate bowl.

Cream Sauce: Melt butter in medium size saucepan. Mix in flour, salt and pepper. Stir in milk until it boils and thickens.

Remove from heat. Whisk in egg. Set aside.

Layer in bread crust as follows:
1. ¹/₂ cup (125 mL) Gruyère cheese
2. ¹/₂ tomato sauce
3. Eggplant
4. ¹/₂ tomato sauce
5. Zucchini
6. Cream sauce
7. ¹/₄ cup (60 mL) Gruyère cheese

Bake in 400°F (200°C) oven for about 40 minutes until hot and crust is browned. Makes 8 medium servings. Make 2 pies for larger helpings.

Pictured on cover.

If you pick a four-leaf clover from poison ivy you are bound to have a rash of good luck.

◀▮▮▮VEAL CUTLETS IN WINE SAUCE

Always popular.

Veal cutlets, about 8 oz. (230 g) each	8	8
Margarine (butter browns too fast)	2 tbsp.	30 mL
Salt, sprinkle		
Pepper, sprinkle		
WINE SAUCE		
Butter or margarine	$^{1}/_{4}$ cup	60 mL
All-purpose flour	$^{1}/_{4}$ cup	60 mL
Salt	$^{1}/_{2}$ tsp.	2 mL
Pepper	$^{1}/_{16}$ tsp.	0.5 mL
Beef bouillon powder	1 tbsp.	15 mL
Milk	2 cups	450 mL
White wine (or alcohol-free wine)	$^{1}/_{4}$ cup	60 mL

Cook veal cutlets in margarine in frying pan. Brown both sides well. Sprinkle with salt and pepper. Add more margarine as needed. Transfer to another container to keep warm.

Wine Sauce: Melt butter in same frying pan. Mix in flour, salt, pepper and bouillon powder. Stir in milk and wine until it boils and thickens. Spoon 2 tbsp. (30 mL) sauce onto center of 8 warm dinner plates. Place veal cutlet on top. Divide remaining sauce over top. Serves 8.

 Germany

1. Sweet Pepper Soup page 58
2. Hot Potato Salad page 64
3. Meatballs page 62
4. Späetzle page 63
5. Red Cabbage page 64
6. Rouladen page 61
7. Sauerkraut page 65

This elegant dessert is also known as Floating Island. In France it is better known as Snow Eggs.

CARAMEL TOPPING

Granulated sugar	1 cup	250 mL
Water	²/₃ cup	150 mL

CUSTARD

Milk	4 cups	900 mL
Egg yolks	8	8
Granulated sugar	³/₄ cup	175 mL
Vanilla	1 tsp.	5 mL

MERINGUE EGGS

Egg whites, room temperature	8	8
Granulated sugar	¹/₃ cup	75 mL
Granulated sugar	1 cup	250 mL

Caramel Topping: Combine sugar and water in small frying pan. Cook over medium-low heat until melted. Continue cooking until deep caramel color. Pour onto greased tray or cake pan. Cool. Grind to a powder in blender.

Custard: Bring milk to a boil in large saucepan.

Whisk egg yolks, sugar and vanilla together in small bowl. Stir a little hot milk into mixture then add to boiling milk. Cook and stir just until it begins to boil. Remove from heat. Strain into serving bowl.

Meringue Eggs: Fill a large pot half full of water and bring to a boil. Reduce heat so water stays just below boiling. Meanwhile beat egg whites in large mixing bowl until stiff. Gradually add first amount of sugar beating continually.

Fold in remaining sugar with rubber spatula. Use 2 metal spoons to shape meringue. Dip spoon into the water, shape meringue by transferring it from one spoon to another to make it round and smooth. Drop into hot water. Repeat, cooking 2 or 3 at the same time. Shape as many meringues as can fit into water in pot. Tops will feel a bit dry after about 15 to 20 seconds. Turn. Let poach for about 30 seconds until firm. Turn at half time. Remove with slotted spoon to paper towels to dry. To serve, pour custard into 8 bowls. Top with eggs (islands). Sprinkle with caramel topping. Serves 8.

Pictured on cover.

STRAWBERRY CREAM CAKE

Strawberries in a custard filling go well with a chocolate crumb crust. Best served the same day it is made.

CRUST

Butter or margarine	⅓ cup	75 mL
Graham cracker crumbs	1½ cups	350 mL
Granulated sugar	2 tbsp.	30 mL
Cocoa	2 tbsp.	30 mL

FILLING

Milk	1½ cups	350 mL
Unflavored gelatin powder	¼ oz.	7 g
Granulated sugar	⅓ cup	75 mL
All-purpose flour	1 tbsp.	15 mL
Salt	¼ tsp.	1 mL
Eggs	2	2
Vanilla	1 tsp.	5 mL
Whipping cream	1 cup	250 mL
Strawberries, cut small	1½ cups	375 mL
Reserved crumbs		

Crust: Melt butter in medium saucepan. Stir in cracker crumbs, sugar and cocoa until moistened. Measure ⅓ cup (75 mL) and reserve for topping. Press the remainder into ungreased 8 inch (20 cm) springform pan. Bake in 350°F (180°C) oven for 10 minutes. Cool.

Filling: Pour milk into saucepan. Sprinkle gelatin over top. Let stand 5 minutes. Place over medium heat. Stir often as you bring it to a boil.

Combine next 5 ingredients in small bowl. Mix well. Stir into boiling milk until it returns to a boil and thickens slightly. Remove from heat. Cover to prevent skin from forming. Chill until it shows signs of setting.

Beat cream in small mixing bowl until thick. Fold into filling.

Fold in strawberries. Turn into prepared pan.

Sprinkle with reserved crumbs. Chill. Serves 8.

GERMANY

Germany is a modern industrial nation in a fairy-tale setting of castles and forests. Boisterous beer gardens alive with song and dance, Christmas tradition, fine German wine and schnapps, finest of automobiles, and high technology are all images of a nation where even pleasure is taken seriously.

German food is substantial and satisfying. It is similar to its neighboring countries, and menus vary depending upon which part of Germany you are visiting.

Unusual combinations such as apples, onions and cabbage make eating in Germany a pleasant adventure. Southern Germany lays claim to the renowned späetzle but the sausage, a true German masterpiece, is a national food.

Meals usually begin with a hearty soup. Less formal meals omit the soup. Delicious, dark bread most often accompanies the meal.

Treat your family and guests to German tradition. Eat Hearty!

MENU 1

*Sweet Pepper Soup   Page 58
Wilted Lettuce   Page 59
*Meatballs   Page 62
*Hot Potato Salad   Page 64 *or*
*Späetzle   Page 63
Red Cabbage   Page 64
Orange Bavarian   Page 67
Coffee   Tea

MENU 2

Chicken Soup   Page 58
Bean Sprout Salad   Page 60
Rouladen   Page 61 *or*
Bratwurst   Page 60
Boiled Salt Potatoes   Page 63
*Sauerkraut   Page 65
German Cheesecake   Page 66
Coffee   Tea

*Pictured page 53

SWEET PEPPER SOUP

A colorful and delicious soup.

Chopped medium red peppers (about 10)	7 cups	1.75 L
Chopped onion	2 cups	500 mL
Chicken bouillon powder	¼ cup	60 mL
Water	2 cups	500 mL
Milk	3½ cups	800 mL
Salt	1 tsp.	5 mL
Pepper	¼ tsp.	1 mL
Thyme	¼ tsp.	1 mL
Cornstarch	2 tbsp.	30 mL
Water	3 tbsp.	50 mL

Combine first 4 ingredients in saucepan. Cover. Simmer until tender. Do not drain. Cool a bit then run through blender.

Combine milk, salt, pepper and thyme in large saucepan. Bring to a boil. Add red pepper mixture. Return to a boil.

Mix cornstarch and remaining water together in small bowl. Stir into boiling soup until it boils again and thickens. Serves 8 people 1 generous cup (250 mL) each.

Pictured on page 53.

CHICKEN SOUP

Served with cooked egg strips in the broth.

Small chicken, cut up	2 lbs.	1 kg
Large onion, cut up	1	1
Large carrot, cut up	1	1
Large parsnip, cut up	1	1
Seasoned salt	2 tbsp.	30 mL
Water	16 cups	3.6 L
Fine egg noodles, broken in short lengths	4 oz.	125 g
Thinly sliced carrots	1 cup	250 mL
Parsley flakes	1 tsp.	5 mL

(continued on next page)

Butter or margarine	3 tbsp.	50 mL
Eggs, lightly beaten	4	4
Salt, sprinkle		
Pepper, sprinkle		

Chopped cooked chicken

Combine first 6 ingredients in large pot. Bring to a boil. Boil covered for about 2 hours. Strain broth into container and return to pot. Discard strainer contents. Reserve chicken. Remove and discard bones. Chop chicken meat and set aside in bowl.

Add egg noodles, second amount of carrots and parsley to broth. Bring to a boil. Boil uncovered until noodles and carrots are tender.

Heat butter in frying pan. Add beaten eggs. Sprinkle with salt and pepper. Cook slowly without stirring. When cooked, cut in strips or squares. Add to soup.

Add chicken. Return to a boil. Serves 8 people 1 cup (250 mL) each.

WILTED LETTUCE.〰

Guests are apt to make a meal of this. The best.

Leaf lettuce, cut or torn, lightly packed	8 cups	2 L
Bacon slices, diced	6	6
Vinegar	1/4 cup	60 mL
Brown sugar, packed	1/4 cup	60 mL
Salt	1/4 tsp.	1 mL
Onion powder	1/4 tsp.	1 mL

Place cut lettuce in large bowl.

Fry bacon in frying pan until crisp.

Add vinegar, brown sugar, salt and onion powder to bacon. Bring to a boil. Immediately pour over lettuce. Toss to coat. Serve while still warm. Serves 8.

BEAN SPROUT SALAD

Enjoy fresh sprouts in a different fashion. A slight curry flavor in the dressing is an excellent touch.

Fresh bean sprouts	2 × 12 oz.	2 × 350 g
Green onions, sliced	6	6
Peeled and diced cucumbers	$1/2$ cup	125 mL
DRESSING		
Mayonnaise	$2/3$ cup	175 mL
Soy sauce	3 tbsp.	50 mL
Vinegar	1 tbsp.	15 mL
Granulated sugar	1 tbsp.	15 mL
Curry powder	$1^1/2$ tsp.	7 mL
Salt	$1/2$ tsp.	2 mL
Ginger	$1/4$ tsp.	1 mL
Sesame seeds, toasted	$1/4$ cup	50 mL
Chopped parsley	2 tbsp.	30 mL

Combine bean sprouts, green onions and cucumber in large bowl.

Dressing: Mix all 7 ingredients together in small bowl. Stir well. Pour over bean sprout mixture. Toss.

Sprinkle with sesame seeds and parsley. Makes 8 generous servings.

BRATWURST

Everyone knows of this German sausage. Quick and easy to prepare.

Bratwurst sausages	$4^1/4$ lbs.	2 kg
Boiling water		
Cooking oil	2 tbsp.	30 mL
Prepared mustard		

Place bratwurst in large pot. Add boiling water to cover. Boil for 5 minutes. This will partially cook sausages and prevent them from bursting. If you buy precooked bratwurst omit this step.

Heat cooking oil in frying pan. Add bratwurst. Cook and brown all sides.

Serve mustard on the side. Serves 8.

When cutting into these rolls, you'll find dill pickle as well as onion and bacon.

Pieces of thinly sliced round steak	8	8
Salt, sprinkle		
Pepper, sprinkle		
Bacon slices, halved crosswise	8	8
Large onions, halved and sliced	1-2	1-2
Medium green peppers cut in strips	1-2	1-2
Large dill pickles, quartered lengthwise	2	2
All-purpose flour for coating	1/4 cup	50 mL
Margarine (butter browns too fast)	2 tbsp.	30 mL
Butter or margarine	6 tbsp.	100 mL
All-purpose flour	6 tbsp.	100 mL
Beef bouillon powder	2 tbsp.	30 mL
Water	4 cups	1 L
Ketchup	1/4 cup	50 mL

Lay meat slices on flat surface. Sprinkle with salt and pepper. Lay 2 pieces of bacon on top of meat followed by onion, green pepper and a slice of dill pickle. Roll up each steak and tie with string.

Coat rolls with flour. Brown in first amount of margarine in frying pan. Add more margarine if needed. Place rolls in small roaster.

Melt second amount of butter or margarine in frying pan. Mix in second amount of flour and bouillon powder. Stir in water and ketchup until it boils and thickens. Pour over meat in roaster. Cover. Bake in 350°F (180°C) oven until fork tender, about 1 1/2 to 2 hours. Makes 8 servings.

Pictured on page 53.

To find your lost dog, put your ear to a tree and listen to the bark.

MEATBALLS

These meatballs are very soft and moist because they're boiled.

Butter or margarine	3 tbsp.	50 mL
Finely chopped onion	2 cups	500 mL
Dry bread crumbs	1½ cups	375 mL
Eggs	2	2
Anchovy paste (or use 8 anchovies, mashed)	1 tbsp.	15 mL
Water	¼ cup	50 mL
Salt	2 tsp.	10 mL
Pepper	½ tsp.	2 mL
Ground beef	1 lb.	454 g
Ground pork	1 lb.	454 g
Water	5 cups	1.25 mL
Onion powder	½ tsp.	2 mL
Whole clove	1	1
Bay leaf	1	1
Salt	½ tsp.	2 mL
Lemon juice	2 tsp.	10 mL

Melt butter in frying pan. Add onion. Sauté until soft and clear. Transfer to bowl.

Add next 6 ingredients to bowl. Mix well.

Add beef and pork. Mix thoroughly. Shape into 2 inch (5 cm) balls. An ice cream scoop works well.

Combine next 6 ingredients in a large saucepan or Dutch oven . Bring to a boil. Using a slotted spoon lower meatballs to bottom of pan. Arrange side by side. Return to a boil. Boil gently until they rise to the top, about 20 minutes. Turn at half time. Remove with slotted spoon to bowl. Keep warm in 250°F (120°C) oven while second batch boils. Measure liquid left in saucepan. Add or remove water, as necessary, to make 2 cups (500 mL) liquid in saucepan.

GRAVY		
All-purpose flour	¼ cup	50 mL
Water	½ cup	125 mL

(continued on next page)

Mix flour and water together until smooth. Stir into cooking liquid in saucepan. Bring to a boil to thicken. Add a bit more water if too thick. Return meatballs to gravy. Makes about 2 dozen. Serves 8 people 3 meatballs each.

Pictured on page 53.

SPÄETZLE

A noodle dough cooked in small pieces. From southern Germany.

Eggs	5	5
All-purpose flour	5 cups	1.13 L
Salt	1³/₄ tsp.	9 mL
Water	1²/₃ cup	375 mL
Butter or margarine	6 tbsp.	100 mL
Finely chopped onion	1 cup	250 mL

In medium bowl beat eggs until frothy. Add flour, salt and water. Beat well. Batter should be too thick to pour from a spoon. Drop teaspoonfuls of batter into pot of boiling water. When they rise to the top cook 1 or 2 minutes more. Remove with slotted spoon to bowl. Keep hot.

Melt butter in frying pan. Add onion. Sauté until soft and clear. Add to späetzle. Toss. Serves 8.

Pictured on page 53.

BOILED SALT POTATOES

Simple and good.

Medium potatoes, peeled, cut in equal size wedges	8	8
Salt	4 tsp.	20 mL
Water	4 cups	1 L
Butter or margarine (optional)	3 tbsp.	50 mL
Parsley flakes (optional)	¹/₂ tsp.	2 mL

Cook potatoes in salt and water until tender. Drain. Return to heat. Shake pot to dry.

Add butter and parsley. Shake pot to melt butter and coat potatoes with both butter and parsley. Serves 8.

HOT POTATO SALAD

Young or waxy potatoes work best with this although any will do. Just toss gently for a neat dish.

Medium potatoes, with peel	8	8
Boiling water		
Bacon slices, diced	10	10
Chopped onion	1 cup	250 mL
Chopped celery	1/2 cup	125 mL
All-purpose flour	2 tbsp.	30 mL
Salt	1 tsp.	5 mL
Pepper	1/4 tsp.	1 mL
Granulated sugar	2 tbsp.	30 mL
Water	2/3 cup	150 mL
Vinegar	1/4 cup	60 mL

Cook potatoes in boiling salted water until tender when pierced with sharp knife point.

Meanwhile combine bacon, onion and celery in frying pan. Sauté until cooked but not colored.

Add flour, salt, pepper and sugar to bacon mixture. Mix well. Stir in water and vinegar. Drain potatoes. Peel. Dice into large bowl. Add bacon mixture. Toss. If you would like a bit more zing, drizzle with more vinegar and toss again. Serves 8.

Pictured on page 53.

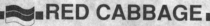
RED CABBAGE

Perfect addition to bratwurst.

Butter or margarine	1/4 cup	50 mL
Chopped onion	1 cup	250 mL
Medium red cabbage, very thinly sliced	2 lbs.	900 g
Cooking apples, peeled and diced	3	3
Brown sugar, packed	1/3 cup	75 mL
Cider vinegar	1/4 cup	50 mL
Water	1/4 cup	50 mL
Whole allspice	3	3
Whole clove	1	1

(continued on next page)

| Salt | 1½ tsp. | 7 mL |
| Pepper | ¼ tsp. | 1 mL |

Melt butter in heavy saucepan. Add onion. Sauté until soft.

Add next 7 ingredients. Bring to a boil. Simmer covered until tender, about 15 minutes.

Add salt and pepper. Stir. Serves 8.

Pictured on page 53.

SAUERKRAUT

A famous German dish. Serve with bratwurst or any meat.

Bacon slices, diced	8	8
Chopped onion	1½ cups	375 mL
Water	2 cups	500 mL
Sauerkraut, drained	2 × 14 oz.	2 × 398 mL
White wine (or alcohol-free wine)	½ cup	125 mL
Medium potato, peeled and grated	1	1
Granulated sugar	2 tsp.	10 mL
Pepper	⅛ tsp.	0.5 mL
Coriander seeds	2	2

Sauté bacon and onion in large saucepan until onion is soft and bacon is cooked.

Add remaining ingredients. Cover and bring to a boil. Boil gently for about 30 minutes. Drain. Serves 8.

Pictured on page 53.

Too bad the nuclear scientist swallowed some uranium. Now he has atomic ache.

GERMAN CHEESECAKE

Very different. Not a sweet cheesecake but dense enough to expect it to be very rich. Made with quark cheese rather than cream cheese.

CRUST

All-purpose flour	²/₃ cup	150 mL
Granulated sugar	¹/₂ cup	125 mL
Baking powder	1 tsp.	5 mL
Egg	1	1
Butter or margarine	6 tbsp.	100 mL

FILLING

Quark cheese, softened	4 cups	1 L
Egg yolks	3	3
Lemon flavoring	1 tsp.	5 mL
Granulated sugar	1 cup	250 mL
Vanilla pudding powder, 4 serving size (not instant)	1	1
Raisins	³/₄ cup	175 mL
Egg whites, room temperature	3	3

Crust: Mix all 5 ingredients well. Press into bottom of ungreased 9 inch (22 cm) springform pan. Set aside.

Filling: Beat cheese, egg yolks and lemon flavoring together in mixing bowl.

Mix in sugar, pudding powder and raisins.

Beat egg whites with clean beaters until stiff. Fold into cheese mixture. Pour into prepared pan. Bake in 350°F (180°C) oven for 60 to 70 minutes until set. Top will be quite brown. Serves 8 generously.

Cross a monster and a cat and you would have a town without any dogs.

Cool and smooth. A nice light dessert.

Unflavored gelatin powder	2 x ¼ oz.	2 x 7 g
Water	½ cup	125 mL
Frozen condensed orange juice	1 cup	225 mL
Water	1 cup	225 mL
Egg yolks	4	4
Granulated sugar	⅔ cup	150 mL
Egg whites, room temperature	4	4
Whipping cream	2 cups	500 mL
Orange slices for garnish		

Sprinkle gelatin over first amount of water in medium saucepan. Let stand for 5 minutes. Place over medium heat.

Add condensed orange juice and second amount of water. Bring to a boil stirring often.

Beat egg yolks and sugar together with spoon. Stir into boiling orange juice mixture. Remove from heat. Stir until sugar is dissolved. Turn into large bowl. Chill until it shows signs of thickening.

In small mixing bowl beat egg whites until stiff. Fold into gelatin mixture.

Beat cream until stiff. Fold into gelatin mixture. Pour into 8 cup (2 L) mold. Chill for several hours. Unmold.

Garnish with orange segments. Serves 8.

How can a bicycle stand up when it is too tired?

GREAT BRITAIN

This picturesque island of green, rolling hills, Scottish highlands, rugged coastlines, castles and noble residences, is the home of Shakespeare and Charles Dickens, Welsh songs, Picadilly Circus, Big Ben, and, of course, the famous cup o' tea, and fish 'n chips.

Think about a meal from Great Britain and roast beef, Yorkshire pudding, and trifle immediately come to mind. However, a great variety of food is available. Lamb and pork are common because they are produced locally and fish is abundant. The British produce their own cheese and have access to a variety of continental European cheeses. Cheese and crackers are often a favorite combination before meals and as dessert.

Charm your family and guests with this taste of Britain!

MENU 1

Mushroom Soup   Page 70
Beetroot Salad   Page 73
Mixed Grill   Page 73 *or*
Glazed Ham   Page 69
Baked Potatoes   Page 76
Minted Peas   Page 78
*Coffee Meringue   Page 80 *or*
Steamed Treacle Pudding   Page 81
Tea   Coffee

MENU 2

Egg Mayonnaise   Page 74
Tomato Rice Salad   Page 74
*Roast Beef   Page 75
*Yorkshire Pudding   Page 76
*Roast Potatoes   Page 77
*Brussels Sprouts   Page 78
Sherry Trifle   Page 79
Tea   Coffee

*Pictured page 71

After being boiled, this ham is glazed in the oven.

Boneless ham	3¹/₂ lbs.	1.6 kg
Water to cover		
Celery sticks, 2 inches (5 cm) in length	8	8
Medium onion quartered	1	1
Whole cloves	6	6
GLAZE		
Canned apricots, halved and pitted	14 oz.	398 mL
Apricot juice and water to make	³/₄ cup	175 mL
Vinegar	2 tbsp.	30 mL
Syrup	2 tbsp.	30 mL
Cloves	¹/₂ tsp.	2 mL
Granulated sugar	¹/₄ cup	60 mL
All-purpose flour	1 tbsp.	15 mL

Place ham in large pot. Add next 4 ingredients. Cover. Bring to a boil. Simmer gently until meat is fork tender, about 1¹/₂ hours. Drain.

Glaze: Drain apricots reserving juice.

Combine apricot juice, vinegar, syrup, cloves, sugar and flour in small saucepan over medium heat. Whisk to blend. Bring to a boil, stirring often. Remove from heat. Place ham in baking pan. Arrange apricot halves around base. Cut most fat from top of ham. Score top in diamond pattern. Baste with glaze. Cook in 400°F (200°C) oven for about 10 to 15 minutes. Baste ham and apricots after 5 minutes with juice. Serves 8.

As one pretzel said to the other pretzel, "Let's twist".

 # MUSHROOM SOUP

An ultra good smooth soup.

Chicken bouillon cubes	4 x 1/5 oz.	4 x 6 g
Boiling water	4 cups	1 L
Chopped onion	1 cup	250 mL
Fresh mushrooms, halved or chunked	1 lb.	454 g
Butter or margarine	6 tbsp.	100 mL
All-purpose flour	6 tbsp.	100 mL
Salt	1 tsp.	5 mL
Pepper	1/4 tsp.	1 mL
Milk	3 cups	750 mL
Whipping cream	8 tbsp.	120 mL

Dissolve bouillon cubes in boiling water in large saucepan.

Add onion and mushrooms. Cover and bring to a boil. Simmer slowly until onions and mushrooms are cooked. Cool slightly. Run through blender.

Melt butter in another large saucepan over medium heat. Mix in flour, salt and pepper.

Stir in milk until it boils and thickens. Add puréed mushroom mixture. Heat through.

Drizzle 1 tbsp. (15 mL) whipping cream over each bowl of soup. Serves 8 people 1 cup (225 mL) each.

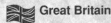 **Great Britain**

1. Coffee Meringue page 80
2. Sherry Trifle page 79
3. Yorkshire Pudding page 76
4. Brussels Sprouts page 78
5. Roast Potatoes page 77
6. Roast Beef with Gravy page 75

BEETROOT SALAD

Except for the color this will remind you a bit of Waldorf salad. Crunchy good.

Canned beets, drained and diced (or use fresh, cooked)	2 × 14 oz.	2 × 398 mL
Sliced celery	1 cup	250 mL
Apple, peeled and diced	1	1
Chopped walnuts	1/4 cup	50 mL
Salt	1/2 tsp.	2 mL
Sour cream	1/4 cup	50 mL
Mayonnaise	1/4 cup	50 mL
Horseradish	1/2 tsp.	2 mL

Combine first 5 ingredients in bowl. Stir to mix.

In small bowl stir sour cream, mayonnaise and horseradish. Add to beet mixture. Toss to coat all ingredients. Serves 8.

MIXED GRILL

Served often in Britain with different variations of meat.

Large sausages	8	8
Boiling water		
Thick lamb chops	8	8
Small fillet steaks	8	8
Bacon slices	8	8
Canadian bacon slices (back bacon)	8	8
Cherry tomatoes	16	16

Cook sausages in boiling water for 5 minutes. Drain. Place on broiler tray. Broil, turning until cooked. Remove to roaster.

Broil or fry lamb chops and fillet steaks. Turn after 10 minutes. When cooked remove to roaster.

Broil bacon. Add to roaster.

Broil cherry tomatoes. Add to roaster. If necessary put roaster in 350°F (180°C) oven until meat is hot. Divide among plates. Serves 8.

EGG MAYONNAISE

A popular starter in the United Kingdom.

Lettuce leaves	8-16	8-16
Hard-boiled eggs, halved lengthwise	8	8
Mayonnaise	1/2 cup	125 mL
Granulated sugar	1 tsp.	5 mL
Lemon juice	1 tsp.	5 mL
Milk	2 tbsp.	30 mL
Paprika, sprinkle		
Parsley, small pieces	16	16

Arrange lettuce on plates. Lay 2 egg halves cut side down on lettuce on each plate.

Mix mayonnaise, sugar, lemon juice and milk together. Spoon over eggs.

Sprinkle with paprika. Top each egg half with a piece of parsley. Serves 8.

TOMATO RICE SALAD

Good and colorful.

Long grain rice	1 cup	250 mL
Boiling salted water	2 cups	500 mL
Tomatoes, peeled and chopped	6	6
Fresh sliced mushrooms	1 cup	250 mL
Green onions, sliced	4	4
Chopped parsley (or 1 tsp. flakes)	2 tbsp.	15 mL
DRESSING		
Cooking oil	1/4 cup	50 mL
Lemon juice	1/4 cup	50 mL
Garlic salt	1/4 tsp.	1 mL
Prepared mustard	1 tsp.	5 mL
Basil	1/2 tsp.	2 mL
Granulated sugar	2 tsp.	10 mL
Salt	1 tsp.	5 mL
Pepper	1/4 tsp.	1 mL

(continued on next page)

Cook rice in boiling salted water until tender and water is absorbed. Rinse with cold water. Drain well.

Dip tomatoes in boiling water until they peel easily, about 1 minute. Combine chopped tomatoes, mushrooms, onion and parsley in large bowl. Add rice. Mix.

Dressing: Mix all 8 ingredients together in small bowl. Pour about $^2/_3$ dressing over salad ingredients. Toss. Add more dressing as needed. Serves 8.

ROAST BEEF

A British tradition. Slices of juicy beef, Yorkshire pudding and gravy will tempt anyone's appetite. Juices are sometimes poured over meat without thickening.

Boned and rolled beef rib roast	**6 lbs.**	**2.7 kg**
(3 ribs from small end of ribs)		
All-purpose flour	**$^1/_3$ cup**	**75 mL**
Water	**4 cups**	**1 L**
Salt	**$^1/_2$ tsp.**	**2 mL**
Pepper	**$^1/_8$ tsp.**	**0.5 mL**
Gravy browner (optional)		
Horseradish		

Place meat in roaster. Cover or leave uncovered if you prefer. Cook in 450°F (230°C) oven for 15 minutes. Turn heat down to 350°F (180°C). Continue to cook until desired degree of doneness, about 15 to 20 minutes per pound (500 g). Serve sliced with horseradish. Serves 8.

Gravy: Remove roast to platter. Keep warm. Remove all the fat you can from roaster. Stir flour into juices in roaster. Brown over medium heat.

Add water, salt and pepper. Stir until it boils and thickens. Add a bit of gravy browner if desired. Taste and add more salt and pepper if needed. Gravy will be thin. Makes about 4 cups (1 L).

Pictured on page 71.

# YORKSHIRE PUDDING

You may want to double this recipe as twelve medium size puffs disappear quickly.

All-purpose flour	1 cup	250 mL
Salt	1/2 tsp.	2 mL
Eggs	2	2
Milk	1 cup	250 mL
Beef drippings or cooking oil	1 tbsp.	15 mL

Combine flour, salt, egg, milk and water in bowl. Beat until smooth, about 5 minutes. Let stand 1 hour.

Pour 1/4 tsp. (1 mL) drippings or cooking oil into each muffin cup. Heat pan in oven. When hot fill cups half full with batter. This is easier to do by pouring batter into pitcher or large measuring cup with pouring lip, then pouring into muffin cups. Bake in 425°F (220°C) top third of oven for about 20 minutes. Makes 12 medium size.

Pictured on page 71.

BAKED POTATOES

Baked and stuffed, these are ready to reheat when needed. Good.

Medium baking potatoes	8	8
Butter or margarine	1 tbsp.	15 mL
Bacon slices, diced	8	8
Sliced fresh mushrooms	2 cups	500 mL
Butter or margarine	1/4 cup	60 mL
Milk	1/2 cup	125 mL
Onion salt	1/2 tsp.	2 mL
Salt	1/2 tsp.	2 mL
Pepper, sprinkle		

For crunchy skins, pierce potatoes in 4 or 5 places and bake. For soft skins pierce and rub with fat or wrap in foil. Bake in 400°F (200°C) oven until tender when poked with tip of sharp paring knife, about 1 hour.

(continued on next page)

Melt first amount of butter in frying pan. Add bacon and mushrooms. Sauté until bacon is cooked. Roll cooked potatoes gently, using potholder to protect hands. Cut off a thin slice from top side. Use a teaspoon to scoop out most of the pulp into bowl.

Add remaining ingredients to potato pulp in bowl. Mash well. Mix in bacon and mushrooms. Stuff potatoes. Bake in 350°F (180°C) oven until hot about 15 minutes. Serves 8.

ROAST POTATOES

Using this method you can have potatoes that are roasted without cooking them with meat.

Medium potatoes, peeled	8	8
Boiling salted water		
Cooking oil	2 tbsp.	30 mL
Margarine	2 tbsp.	30 mL

Cook potatoes in boiling salted water for 10 minutes. Drain. Blot dry.

Meanwhile heat cooking oil in 9 × 13 inch (22 × 33 cm) pan or small roaster. Place potatoes in pan turning each to coat with cooking oil and margarine. Cook covered for about 1 hour until tender. If there is room in roaster when cooking roast, potatoes may be cooked along-side. This is difficult for a large number of guests. Serves 8.

Pictured on page 71.

He isn't a light sleeper. He sleeps in the dark.

BRUSSELS SPROUTS

A different method to finish these delectable sprouts.

Frozen Brussels sprouts	3 × 10 oz.	3 × 300 g
Boiling salted water		
Butter or margarine	½ **cup**	**125 mL**

Cook Brussels sprouts in boiling salted water until tender. Drain.

Melt butter in large heavy pan or Dutch oven. Add Brussels sprouts. Brown, shaking several times. They might start to look as though they are "all shook up" but that's when they're good. Total browning time should be about 7 to 8 minutes. Serves 8.

Pictured on page 71.

MINTED PEAS

With small triangles of fried bread mixed in.

Frozen peas (or fresh)	3 × 10 oz.	3 × 300 g
Boiling salted water		
Sprigs of mint	2	2
Butter or margarine	¼ **cup**	**50 mL**
Cream	2 tbsp.	30 mL
Granulated sugar	2 tsp.	10 mL
Salt	⅛ tsp.	0.5 mL
Cooking oil	1 tbsp.	15 mL
Butter or margarine	1 tbsp.	15 mL
Bread slices, crusts removed	5	5

Cook peas in boiling salted water until tender. Drain.

Add next 5 ingredients to peas. Heat to melt butter. Shake saucepan several times.

Heat cooking oil and butter in frying pan. Fry bread slices browning both sides. Add more butter if needed. Cut each slice corner to corner making 4 triangles. Cut these 4 in half to make 8 triangles per slice. Add to peas. Shake together and turn out into serving bowl. Serves 8.

A grand finale to a meal.

Sponge or pound cake	1	1
Raspberry jam or other red jam	1/3 cup	75 mL
Sherry (or alcohol-free sherry)	1/3 cup	75 mL
CUSTARD		
Milk	3 cups	700 mL
Custard powder	3 tbsp.	50 mL
Granulated sugar	6 tbsp.	100 mL
Salt, scant measure	1/2 tsp.	2 mL
Vanilla	3/4 tsp.	4 mL
Eggs	2	2
TOPPING		
Whipping cream	1 cup	250 mL
Granulated sugar	1 tbsp.	15 mL
Vanilla	1 tsp.	5 mL
Almonds, halved or slivered	2 tbsp.	30 mL
Maraschino cherries	11	11

Cut cake to make 10 slices approximately the size of a deck of cards. Spread 5 slices with jam. Press the other 5 slices over jam. Cut each sandwich into cubes. Place cubes into pretty glass bowl.

Sprinkle sherry over cake. Let stand to absorb.

Custard: Heat milk in heavy saucepan until boiling.

In small bowl combine custard powder, sugar and salt. Stir to mix thoroughly. Add vanilla and eggs. Mix together. Stir into boiling milk until thickened slightly. Remove from heat and cool a few minutes. While it is still quite warm pour over cake. Cover with foil. Chill. The foil will prevent a crust from forming.

Topping: Beat cream, sugar and vanilla until stiff. Spread over chilled custard.

Decorate top with almonds and cherries. Place 8 cherries around outside edge and 3 in center. Serves 8.

Variation: Add sliced sweetened peach slices, canned or fresh. Place among cake cubes.

Pictured on page 71.

# COFFEE MERINGUE

Make this in the morning or at least a few hours ahead. Everyone will wonder how it is made. Allow extra time. Meringues can be made a few days ahead of assembly.

CHOCOLATE MERINGUE

Egg whites, room temperature	2	2
Granulated sugar	1/2 cup	125 mL
Cocoa	3 tbsp.	50 mL

COFFEE MERINGUE

Egg whites, room temperature	2	2
Granulated sugar	1/2 cup	125 mL
Instant coffee granules, crushed to a fine powder	1 tsp.	5 mL

FILLING

Milk	1 1/2 cups	350 mL
Unflavored gelatin powder	1/4 oz.	7 g
Granulated sugar	1/3 cup	75 mL
All-purpose flour	1 tbsp.	15 mL
Egg yolks	4	4
Instant coffee granules, crushed to a fine powder	1 tbsp.	15 mL
Salt	1/4 tsp.	1 mL
Whipping cream	1 cup	250 mL

Chocolate Meringue: Beat egg whites in small mixing bowl until soft peaks hold. Add sugar gradually, beating until very stiff and sugar is dissolved. Fold in cocoa. Lightly grease 8 inch (20 cm) springform pan. Spread with meringue. Smooth top. Bake in 250°F (130°C) oven for about 45 minutes until dry and crispy firm. Turn off heat. Leave in oven for about 2 hours. Cool.

Coffee Meringue: Beat egg whites in small mixing bowl until soft peaks hold. Add sugar and coffee powder gradually, beating until stiff. Mark rings on foil 5 1/2 and 2 1/2 inches (14 and 6 cm) in diameter. Pipe meringue over ring line about 3/4 inch (2 cm) in width. On same pan or another pan pipe remaining meringue in strips any length. Bake in 250°F (130°C) oven for about 45 to 50 minutes until crispy firm and dry. Cool. Remove from foil. If rings break you can put them together when putting in place.

Filling: Pour milk into saucepan. Sprinkle gelatin over top. Let stand 5 minutes. Place over medium heat. Stir to dissolve gelatin. Bring to a boil.

(continued on next page)

Mix sugar and flour in small bowl. Add egg yolks, coffee and salt. Stir well. Add to boiling milk stirring until it returns to a boil and thickens. Remove from heat. Chill covered (so top skin doesn't form) until it begins to set.

Beat cream until stiff. Fold into rest of filling. To assemble, spread meringue with ½ filling. Lay coffee meringues on top. Cover with second ½ filling. Chill. Remove ring from pan. Crumble meringue sticks. Just before serving sprinkle with crumbled meringue. Serves 8.

Pictured on page 71.

STEAMED TREACLE PUDDING

Of the many British steamed puddings this is the most versatile. You can use your favorite sauce of any flavor.

Butter or margarine, softened	1 cup	225 mL
Granulated sugar	1 cup	225 mL
Eggs	4	4
All-purpose flour	2 cups	450 mL
Baking powder	2 tsp.	10 mL
Salt	³/₄ tsp.	4 mL
Golden syrup	¹/₂ cup	125 mL

Cream butter and sugar together. Beat in eggs 1 at a time.

Add flour, baking powder and salt. Stir to mix.

Grease bottom of 2 quart (2.5 mL) pudding pan. Pour syrup into pan. Spoon batter over syrup. Cover with greased foil. Tie in place. Place pudding in steamer with boiling water reaching ³/₄ up the sides of pan. Cover and steam for 2 hours. Check in about 1 hour adding more boiling water to keep level up. To serve, turn pudding out onto warmed serving plate. Pour sauce over top and serve. Serves 8.

SAUCE

Golden syrup	1 cup	250 mL
Water	2 tbsp.	30 mL

Heat syrup and water in small saucepan. Pour over steamed pudding. Makes a generous 1 cup (250 mL).

 # INDIA

India is a mysterious land of extreme wealth and poverty, crowded markets and temples, lonely mystics, beautiful valleys and dry plains. In this land of contrasts, it's not uncommon to see cows wandering in the midst of busy city intersections.

Indian cuisine varies from region to region depending upon availability of ingredients. Rice is a staple food. Bread is not usually eaten with rice. Potatoes are combined with vegetables. Easy to prepare, Indian food combines sweet and savory spices. Visit an Indian food store for hard-to-find or fresh spices.

Enjoy hot, spicy dishes accompanied by yogurt or decrease the amount of spice and simply experience the variety of flavors. Relax at the end of the meal with a cup of fine Indian tea.

Discover the taste sensations of India!

MENU 1

*Samosas   Page 83
Roghan Josh   Page 86 *or*
Chicken Curry   Page 85
Tomato Raita   Page 83
*Yellow Rice   Page 92
Green Beans   Page 91
*Chapati   Page 93
*Carrot Halwa   Page 95
Tea

MENU 2

*Poppadums   Page 84
*Onion Bhajia   Page 84
*Katcha Korma   Page 87 *or*
Vindaloo   Page 91
Tomato Cuke Raita   Page 86
Rice With Lentils   Page 92
*Potato-Cauliflower Bhajia   Page 88
*Puri   Page 94
Gulab Jamuns   Page 94
Tea

*Pictured page 89

Great little tidbits. Good as is or serve with chutney.

Cooking oil	2 tbsp.	30 mL
Chopped onion	2 cups	500 g
Garlic cloves, minced	2	2
Grated ginger	1 tsp.	5 mL
Salt	1 tsp.	5 mL
Cayenne pepper (Indian Chili Powder)	1/2 tsp.	2 mL
Canned broken shrimp, drained	2 x 4 oz.	2 x 113 g
Grated potato	1/2 cup	125 mL
Water	1/4 cup	50 mL
Wonton wrappers	1 lb.	454 g

Fat for deep-frying

Heat cooking oil in frying pan. Add next 5 ingredients. Stir. Sauté until onion is soft.

Add shrimp, potato and water. Cover and cook until potato is tender. If any liquid remains cook uncovered until it is gone. Cool.

Place about 1 tbsp. (15 mL) or less of shrimp mixture in center of wonton wrappers. Moisten sides with water. Fold over in triangle shapes. Press edges to seal.

Deep-fry in hot fat 375°F (190°C) until golden brown on both sides. Remove with slotted spoon to paper towels to drain. Makes about 4 to 4 1/2 dozen.

Pictured on page 89.

TOMATO RAITA

A cooler to serve with spicy-hot food.

Yogurt	3 cups	750 mL
Salt	1 tsp.	5 mL
Pepper, sprinkle		
Paprika	1/2 tsp.	2 mL
Tomatoes, cut bite size	6	6

Combine yogurt, salt, pepper and paprika in bowl. Stir.

Add tomato. Stir to mix. Makes 4 cups (1 L).

~. POPPADUMS

Buy these poppadums or snacks in an Indian grocery store. When deep-fried they puff up increasing in size considerably. Great for munching.

Far Far, potato and rice snack food (Virani's is good)	**8.8 oz.**	**250 g**
Green Chillies Papad	**8.8 oz.**	**250 g**
Cooking oil for deep-frying (not lard, butter or margarine)		

Far Far: These are $^{13}/_{16}$ inch (2 cm) square and very thin. When deep-fried they crunch like popcorn. Colors are pastel when done. Deep-fry in very hot cooking oil 400°F (200°C) for 6 to 8 seconds. Remove with slotted spoon to paper towels to drain. Makes a big bowlful.

Green Chillies Papad: These are paper thin 7 inch (18 cm) circles. When deep-fried they puff up as well. Put 2 thin circles together to deep-fry. This keeps edges straight. Cook on 1 side for about 12 to 14 seconds. Turn both together. Cook for another 12 to 15 seconds. Remove to paper towels to drain. Makes about 19.

Pictured on page 89.

~. ONION BHAJIA

This is India's version of onion rings.

Gram flour	**1 cup**	**225 mL**
Salt	**$^1/_4$ tsp.**	**1 mL**
Baking powder	**$^1/_4$ tsp.**	**1 mL**
Water	**$^2/_3$ cup**	**150 mL**
Large onion, cut in rings and separated	**1**	**1**
Fat for deep-frying		
Mint chutney or taco sauce for dipping		

(continued on next page)

Combine flour, salt and baking powder in bowl. Stir.

Add water and mix. It should be the consistency of pancake batter.

Stir onion rings into batter.

Drop rings separately into hot fat 375°F (190°C). Cook until browned. Drain on paper towels.

Serve with sauce for dipping. Serves 8.

Pictured on page 89.

EGGPLANT BHAJIA: Deep-fry eggplant strips the same way.

CHICKEN CURRY

India is well known for its curries. This recipe is a delicious, potent dish in which the curry content can be lessened if desired.

Cooking oil	$^2/_3$ cup	150 mL
Medium onions, sliced	2	2
Tomato juice	1 cup	250 mL
Water	$^1/_2$ cup	125 mL
Curry powder	3 tbsp.	50 mL
Garlic cloves, minced	3-6	3-6
Salt	1 tbsp.	15 mL
Chopped ginger	2 tbsp.	30 mL
Bay leaves	4	4
Whole cloves	6	6
Whole cardamoms	4	4
Chicken parts, skin removed	6 lbs.	2.72 kg

Heat cooking oil in large Dutch oven. Add onion. Cook until browned.

Add next 9 ingredients. Bring to a boil. Cook uncovered for 5 minutes, stirring often.

Add chicken. Cook uncovered for another 5 minutes. Stir often. Cover and simmer slowly until tender, about 40 minutes. Keep chicken at a gentle simmer. Do not add more water. If it gets dry then you will have to add just a touch. Stir occasionally. Serves 8.

TOMATO CUKE RAITA

Even though this contains cayenne pepper for flavor it still makes a good cooler.

Yogurt	3 cups	750 mL
Cumin	1/2 tsp.	2 mL
Salt	1 tsp.	5 mL
Cayenne pepper (Indian Chili Powder)	1/2 tsp.	2 mL
Medium onion, quartered and thinly sliced	1	1
Cucumber, peeled, halved lengthwise and sliced	1	1
Medium tomato, peeled, quartered and sliced	1	1

Combine first 4 ingredients in bowl. Stir.

Add onion and cucumber. Dip tomato in boiling water for about 1 minute until it peels easily. Cut and add to bowl. Stir together. Makes 5 cups (1.25 L).

ROGHAN JOSH

Although lamb is used in this recipe, beef stew meat is every bit as good.

Lamb stew meat, cubed, or beef stew meat	4 1/4 lbs.	2 kg
Chopped onion	4 cups	1 L
Cooking oil	1/3 cup	75 mL
Salt	4 tsp.	20 mL
Water	1 cup	250 mL
Yogurt	1 1/2 cups	375 mL
Coriander powder	2 1/2 tbsp.	40 mL
Coarsely ground black pepper	4 tsp.	20 mL
Cayenne pepper (Indian Chili Powder)	2 1/2 tsp.	12 mL

(continued on next page)

Ginger	1¼ tsp.	6 mL
Garlic powder	1 tsp.	5 mL
Cinnamon	½ tsp.	2 mL
Cardamom	½ tsp.	2 mL
Cloves	¼ tsp.	1 mL

Combine first 5 ingredients in saucepan. Cover. Bring to a boil. Simmer until all liquid has been used and meat is tender, about 1½ hours. If meat isn't tender add a bit more water and simmer until it is. Meat will then begin to sizzle in the remaining cooking oil.

Add remaining ingredients. Stir. Simmer slowly uncovered until sauce thickens. Serves 8.

KATCHA KORMA.≈

Absolutely delicious.

Beef stew meat, cut bite size	4¼ lbs.	2 kg
Cooking oil	⅓ cup	75 mL
Chopped onion	1½ cups	375 mL
Yogurt	⅓ cup	75 mL
Ground coriander	4 tsp.	20 mL
Salt	4 tsp.	20 mL
Chopped ginger	2½ tbsp.	40 mL
Garlic cloves, minced	4	4
Bay leaves	3	3
Peppercorns	1½ tsp.	7 mL
Whole cloves	8	8
Cinnamon	¼ tsp.	1 mL
Whole cardamoms	3	3
Boiling water	1 cup	250 mL
Beef bouillon cubes, crumbled	1 x ⅕ oz.	1 x 6 g

Measure first 13 ingredients into large saucepan.

Pour boiling water over bouillon cubes in small bowl. Stir to dissolve. Pour over meat in saucepan. Cover and bring to a boil, stirring often. Boil slowly until meat is tender and water has boiled away, about 1½ hours. If necessary add a bit more water. There will still be some cooking oil in saucepan. Brown meat in it until meat is as brown as you desire. Serves 8.

Pictured on page 89.

POTATO-CAULIFLOWER BHAJIA

All vegetables are cooked in one dish. Tiny green chillies may be added to spice it up.

Cooking oil	⅓ cup	75 mL
Chopped onion	1 cup	250 mL
Medium potatoes, peeled and cubed	8	8
Medium-small cauliflower, broken up	1	1
Peas, fresh of frozen	1 cup	250 mL
Medium tomatoes, skin removed and cut up	2	2
Salt	1 tsp.	5 mL
Water	1 cup	250 mL

Heat cooking oil in large saucepan or Dutch oven. Add onion. Sauté until soft and browned.

Add remaining ingredients. Cover and bring to a boil. Boil slowly until vegetables are tender, about 25 minutes. Add a bit more water if necessary but there should be no water left when vegetables are cooked. Serves 8.

Pictured on page 89.

 India

VINDALOO

This is usually a very hot meat dish so heap up the spoon of cayenne if you dare.

Pork stew meat, in cubes	4¼ lbs.	2 kg
Vinegar	1¼ cups	275 mL
Cooking oil	⅓ cup	75 mL
Curry powder	3 tbsp.	50 mL
Granulated sugar	4 tsp.	20 mL
Salt	4 tsp.	20 mL
Cayenne pepper (Indian Chili Powder)	¾ tsp.	4 mL

Combine all ingredients together in large saucepan. Cover. Bring to a boil. Boil slowly until tender, about 1½ hours. Add boiling water in small amounts as needed. Serves 8.

GREEN BEANS

A vegetable dish that is a touch hot.

Cooking oil	2 tbsp.	30 mL
Chopped onion	1½ cups	375 mL
Mustard seed	½ tsp.	2 mL
Ginger	¼ tsp.	1 mL
Frozen cut green beans	3 × 10 oz.	3 × 284 g
Garam marsala	1 tsp.	5 mL
Turmeric	½ tsp.	2 mL
Crushed red chilies	½ tsp.	2 mL
Salt	½ tsp.	2 mL

Heat cooking oil in frying pan. Add onion, mustard seed and ginger. Sauté until onion is soft.

Add remaining ingredients. Stir. Cover to steam for about 8 minutes. Stir-fry until beans are tender crisp. Serves 8.

YELLOW RICE

A cheery yellow color with just the right spices.

Butter or margarine	2 tbsp.	30 mL
Chopped onion	1 cup	250 mL
Basmatic rice (or other long grain)	2¹/₂ cups	625 mL
Water	5 cups	1.25 L
Salt	1 tsp.	5 mL
Cumin seeds	1 tsp.	5 mL
Cardamom seeds	1 tsp.	5 mL
Turmeric	¹/₄ tsp.	1 mL

Melt butter in saucepan. Add onion. Sauté until soft and clear.

Add rice. Sauté for about 2 minutes.

Add remaining ingredients. Stir. Bring to a boil. Simmer covered for about 15 minutes until rice is tender and water is absorbed. Fluff with fork. Serves 8.

Pictured on page 89.

RICE WITH LENTILS

This is a creamy color even though red lentils are added. Contains peas.

Cooking oil	3 tbsp.	50 mL
Whole cardamons	4	4
Small cinnamon stick, 2 inch (5 cm)	1	1
Whole cloves	4	4
Bay leaves	3	3
Medium onions, sliced	3	3
Basmatic rice (or other long grain)	2¹/₂ cups	625 mL
Split red lentils	¹/₂ cup	125 mL
Peas, fresh or frozen	1 cup	250 mL
Water	6 cups	1.5 mL
Salt	1 tbsp.	15 mL
Chicken bouillon powder	1 tbsp.	15 mL

(continued on next page)

Heat oil in large saucepan. Add next 5 ingredients. Sauté until onions are soft.

Add rice and lentils. Sauté for 3 minutes, stirring often.

Add remaining ingredients. Bring to a boil. Simmer covered until tender and water is absorbed, about 15 minutes. Discard bay leaf. Fluff with fork. Serves 8.

CHAPATI

An East Indian bread served with meals. It is not usually eaten at the same time as rice or potatoes.

Whole wheat flour	3 cups	700 mL
Salt	1 tsp.	5 mL
Water	1 ⅛ cups	250 mL
Butter or margarine, melted	¼ cup	60 mL

Measure flour and salt into bowl. Mix. Add water. Stir together to make firm dough. Add a bit more water if needed. Knead on lightly floured surface until smooth and not too dry. Cover with plastic wrap. Let stand 30 minutes. Roll in cylinder shape. Mark then cut into 16 pieces. Form each into a patty then roll out very thin. Roll out all 16 pieces before cooking. They cook too fast to roll them while cooking. To cook, heat frying pan medium-hot. Place 1 chapati in pan. Press around edges to make more bubbles form. Brown spots will appear on the underside. Turn. When brown spots have appeared on second side remove to tray.

Brush with melted butter. Keep warm by covering with towel or hold in 225°F (140°C) oven while frying the remaining rounds. Makes 16.

Pictured on page 89.

Paré Pointer

The letter was damp. The postage was dew.

PURI

It is easy to make this East Indian bread. Served with meals but not usually eaten with potatoes or rice. Puffy.

Whole wheat flour	1¹/₂ cups	350 mL
All-purpose flour	1¹/₂ cups	350 mL
Salt	1 tsp.	5 mL
Cooking oil	2 tbsp.	30 mL
Hot water	1¹/₄ cups	275 mL

Fat for deep-frying

Measure both flours and salt into bowl. Mix. Add cooking oil and water. Stir together to form a fairly stiff dough. Add a bit more water if needed. Knead on lightly floured surface until smooth and springy. Pinch off small golf ball size pieces or smaller. Press into patties. Roll very thin.

Deep-fry in 375° F (180° C) fat to brown both sides. Makes about 30.

Pictured on page 89.

GULAB JAMUNS

These little balls are a delightful surprise. After deep-frying very slowly they are soaked for a brief period in a light syrup.

SYRUP		
Granulated sugar	4 cups	1 L
Water	4 cups	1 L
BALLS		
Skim milk powder	4 cups	1 L
All-purpose flour	1 cup	250 mL
Baking powder	2 tsp.	10 mL
Butter or margarine	¹/₄ cup	60 mL
Evaporated milk	1 ³/₄ cup	425 mL

Fat for deep-frying

Syrup: Combine sugar and water in medium saucepan. Heat and stir until boiling and sugar is dissolved. Turn heat down so syrup will keep warm but not cook.

(continued on next page)

Balls: Combine milk powder, flour and baking powder in bowl. Cut in butter until mixture is crumbly.

Add evaporated milk. Mix well. Dough will be firm. Shape into 1 inch (2.5 cm) balls.

Heat fat to 300°F (150°C). Slowly deep-fry balls until brown. Remove with slotted spoon. Drain on paper towels for a few moments then put them in syrup for 5 minutes. Remove from syrup onto plate. Makes about 4½ to 5 dozen.

CARROT HALWA.

A colorful rich dessert.

Grated carrot	**6 cups**	**1.5 L**
Milk	**3 cups**	**750 mL**
Ground cardamom	**1½ tsp.**	**7 mL**
Granulated sugar	**1¾ cup**	**425 mL**
Butter or margarine	**½ cup**	**125 mL**
Almonds for garnish	**1½ tbsp.**	**25 mL**
Pistachios for garnish	**1½ tbsp.**	**25 mL**
Whipping cream	**1½ cups**	**375 mL**

Combine carrot, milk and cardamom into large heavy saucepan. Cook uncovered over medium heat, stirring often. Cook until liquid is almost gone.

Stir in sugar. Continue to cook until there is no liquid left.

Add butter. Fry and stir until mixture turns a darker rich color, about 10 to 15 minutes or more. Turn into bowl.

Garnish with nuts that have been slivered, chopped or ground. If serving cold, spread in greased 9 x 9 inch (22 x 22 cm) pan. Cut into triangles.

Serve lightly whipped cream on the side, or pour just as is over top. Serves 8.

Pictured on page 89.

 **ITALY**

From snow-covered Alps in the north to warm, rocky shores of the south, Italy is rich in history, culture and contrast. Roman emperors and guests, with their passions for art, music, fine food and wine, feasted at lavish banquets. Today, Italians maintain these passions and have also managed to maintain their own culinary style. And, as if that's not enough... Italian food is good for you!

Begin the day with a cup of cappuccino, enjoy rich black expresso at midday or sit in the sun and sip on sturdy Italian wine accompanied by Italian bread and excellent cheese.

Entertain in the formal Italian style, serving several courses: 1) antipasto, 2) thin soup, 3) pasta or rice, 4) meat or fish, 5) salad, 6) dessert, 7) expresso or cappuccino. For every-day dining, serve a three-course meal. Begin with antipasto or soup. Then set the table with bowls of pasta, meat with red tomato sauce (traditional in the south) or rice with fish and white cream sauce (standard in the north), and vegetables. Let everyone help themselves. You may want to serve cheese and fruit which are usual desserts, or present a scrumptious Italian cake.

Salute (sal-LOO-tay) and welcome to sunny Italy!

MENU 1

*Antipasto   Page 98
*Stuffed Eggs   Page 98
Meat Sauced Spaghetti   Page 109
Chicken Scalloppine   Page 102 *or*
Veal Marsala   Page 101 *or*
Tomato Sole   Page 105
Sweet And Sour Carrots   Page 105
*Tomato Cheese Salad   Page 100
*Cassata Alla Siciliana   Page 112
Expresso

MENU 2

*Fried Mozzarella   Page 99 *or*
Tomato Cream Soup   Page 97
*Osso Buco   Page 103
*Risotta Milanese   Page 104
Zucchini Casserole   Page 110
Artichoke Salad   Page 100 *or*
Mixed Salad   Page 106
*Zabaglione   Page 113 *or*
Italian Cheesecake   Page 111
Expresso

*Pictured page 107

A very tomato soup with vegetables.

Butter or margarine	3 tbsp.	50 mL
Chopped onion	1 cup	250 mL
Diced carrot	1 cup	250 mL
Tomatoes, quartered	4	4
Sliced celery	$^1/_2$ cup	125 mL
Condensed chicken broth	2 × 10 oz.	2 × 284 mL
Tomato sauce	$7^1/_2$ oz.	213 mL
Granulated sugar	1 tbsp.	15 mL
Whole black peppercorns	12	12
Salt	2 tsp.	10 mL
Parsley flakes	$^1/_2$ tsp.	2 mL
Beef bouillon cube, crushed	$^1/_5$ oz.	6 g
Boiling water	$1^1/_4$ cup	275 mL
Cream	$^3/_4$ cup	175 mL

Melt butter in large saucepan. Add onion and carrot. Sauté until soft.

Dip tomatoes into boiling water for about 1 minute until they peel easily. Peel and cut. Add next 8 ingredients.

Dissolve bouillon cube in boiling water. Add to soup. Cover and simmer for 30 minutes.

To serve, add cream and pour into soup bowls. Serves 8 people about 1 cup (225 mL) each.

Humpty Dumpty had a great fall. Too bad his summer was so bad.

STUFFED EGGS

Eggs brighten an antipasto tray. These have a bit darker stuffing due to the addition of anchovy paste.

Hard-boiled eggs, halved lengthwise	8	8
Anchovy paste	1¹/₂ tsp.	7 mL
Olive oil or cooking oil	2 tbsp.	30 mL
Parsley flakes	¹/₄ tsp.	1 mL
Garlic powder	¹/₈ tsp.	0.5 mL
Prepared mustard	¹/₄ tsp.	1 mL
Salt	¹/₈ tsp.	0.5 mL
Pepper, light sprinkle		
Salad dressing (Miracle Whip is good)		
Pimiento stuffed olives, sliced	4	4

Carefully remove egg yolks from whites. Place yolks in bowl and mash with fork.

Add next 7 ingredients. Mash together. If too dry add more olive oil. Fill egg whites.

Put a dab of salad dressing on each. Top with olive slice. Arrange on antipasto tray. Makes 16.

Pictured on page 107.

ANTIPASTO

An Italian favorite appetizer. This may be served in the living room before the meal or at the dining room table.

Prosciutto or ham slices	8	8
Genoa salami slices	8	8
Provolone cheese slices, or other	8	8
Mortadella slices	8	8
Canned artichoke hearts, drained	14 oz.	398 mL
Black olives	16	16
Green olives	16	16
Honeydew	8	8
Canteloupe slices	8	8
Stuffed eggs, see page 98	16	16

(continued on next page)

Fill a platter with all or some of the listed selection. Arrange in a nice pattern. Cut large meat slices. Roll up to arrange on platter. Serve as a first course. Allow people to serve themselves. Serves 8.

Pictured on page 107.

FRIED MOZZARELLA

Strips or triangles of cheese deep-fried with a crumb coating. Just delicious.

Mozzarella cheese slices	16	16
All-purpose flour	$^1/_3$ cup	75 mL
Eggs	2	2
Water	4 tsp.	20 mL
Salt	$^1/_4$ tsp.	1 mL
Pepper	$^1/_{16}$ tsp.	0.5 mL
Dry fine breadcrumbs	1 cup	250 mL
Fat for deep-frying		
Black olives	8	8
Green olives	8	8
Parsley sprigs	8	8

Separate cheese slices into groups of 4, keeping slices in each group tight together. Cut each group in half through center then in half again making 4 thick strips. Repeat with other groups of cheese, making 16 strips in all. A solid piece of Mozzarella may be used instead. Try to cut uniform slices. Triangles may be made by cutting cornerwise.

Measure flour into flat dish.

Combine eggs, water, salt and pepper in cereal bowl. Beat with fork until blended.

Measure breadcrumbs into another flat dish. Dip cheese strips in flour. Dip in egg, then in breadcrumbs. Be sure every spot is covered with crumbs. Line with waxed paper a pan large enough to hold cheese in single layer. Lay cheese on waxed paper. Chill for 1 hour or more.

Gently fry a few cheese strips at a time in hot 375°F (190°C) fat, browning both sides. Remove with slotted spoon to drain on paper towels. Place 2 strips on each plate.

Add 1 black olive, 1 green olive and 1 sprig of parsley to each plate. Serves 8.

Pictured on page 107.

TOMATO CHEESE SALAD

Attractive as well as easy.

Tomatoes, seeded and cut bite size	8	8
Mozzarella cheese, diced	$^1/_2$ lb.	250 g
Black olives	16-24	16-24
Basil	$^1/_2$ tsp.	2 mL
Olive oil or cooking oil	$^1/_4$ cup	50 mL
Salt, sprinkle		
Pepper, sprinkle		
Lettuce leaves	3-4	3-4

Combine tomato, cheese, olives and basil in bowl. Stir.

Add olive oil and toss. Sprinkle with salt and pepper. Toss. Add more salt and pepper as needed.

Line large plate with lettuce leaves. Arrange salad on top. Serves 8.

Picture on page 107.

ARTICHOKE SALAD

Delicate looking and unusual.

Assorted lettuce leaves, frilly, leaf, head, romaine	24	24
Radiccio leaves	8	8
Endive leaves	8	8
Alfalfa sprouts	2 × 5 oz.	2 × 135 g
Canned artichoke hearts, quartered	2 × 14 oz.	2 × 398 mL
Diced red pepper	2 tbsp.	30 mL
Diced green pepper	2 tbsp.	30 mL
Diced yellow pepper	2 tbsp.	30 mL
Hard-boiled eggs, sliced	3	3
Creamy Italian dressing or creamy vinaigrette		

(continued on next page)

Cover 6 salad plates with a variety of green leaves. Try to add a leaf of radiccio and endive to each plate for interest.

Divide alfalfa sprouts onto center of each plate. Spread to form level cushion. Spoon artichoke pieces over sprouts. Sprinkle with diced peppers. Arrange about 2 egg slices on side of salad.

Drizzle with dressing or serve on the side. Serves 6.

VEAL MARSALA

So tender and full of flavor. After steak is cooked it is simmered in a wine and mushroom mixture.

Margarine (butter browns too fast)	2 tbsp.	30 mL
Veal sirloin steak	5 lbs.	2.27 kg
All-purpose flour	$^2/_3$ cup	150 mL
Salt, sprinkle		
Pepper, sprinkle		
Marsala wine or sherry (or alcohol-free sherry)	1 cup	250 mL
Water	1 cup	250 mL
Beef bouillon powder	2 tsp.	10 mL
Canned sliced mushrooms, drained (optional)	2 × 10 oz.	2 × 284 mL

Melt margarine in frying pan.

Dredge steak in flour. Fry immediately after coating with flour to cook and brown both sides. Add more margarine as needed.

Remove cooked steaks to platter. Sprinkle with salt and pepper.

Add marsala and water to empty pan. Stir to loosen any bits that are stuck on pan. Add bouillon powder and mushrooms. Stir. Return steaks a few at a time to frying pan. Heat steaks in simmering sauce for 3 minutes, turning once. Transfer to platter in warm oven. Repeat. Pour sauce over steaks on platter. Serves 8.

A take off from veal scalloppine.

Large chicken breasts, halved, skinned and boned (or turkey cutlets)	4	4
All-purpose flour	$1/2$ cup	125 mL
Margarine (butter browns too fast)	2 tbsp.	30 mL
Garlic powder	$1/8$ tsp.	0.5 mL
Chicken bouillon powder	1 tsp.	5 mL
Prosciutto ham slices to fit	8	8
Mozzarella cheese slices to fit	8	8

Dip chicken in flour to coat. If you'd rather use veal, pound with meat mallet before coating with flour.

Melt margarine in frying pan. Stir in garlic powder and bouillon powder. Fry about $1/2$ of chicken until cooked and browned on both sides. To fry second $1/2$ of chicken mix more margarine, garlic powder and bouillon together in pan as in the beginning then add rest of chicken. Arrange chicken on tray or broiler pan.

Lay slice of ham over each portion. Lay slice of cheese over ham. Broil close to heat until cheese is melted and browned. Spoon sauce over each serving. Makes 8 servings.

SAUCE

Marsala wine or sherry (or alcohol-free sherry)	3 tbsp.	50 mL
White wine (or alcohol-free wine)	3 tbsp.	50 mL
Water	1 cup	250 mL
Chicken bouillon powder	1 tbsp.	15 mL
Cornstarch	2 tbsp.	30 mL

Sauce: Measure all ingredients into small saucepan. Mix well. Stir over medium heat until it boils and thickens. Spoon over meat or serve on the side. Makes 1 cup (250 mL).

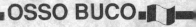

A well known Italian meal that is accompanied by Rissoto Milanese.
Gravy is excellent.

All-purpose flour	1 cup	250 mL
Salt	2 tsp.	10 mL
Pepper	1/2 tsp.	2 mL
Veal hind shanks, cut in 2 inch (5 cm) lengths	3	3
Margarine (butter browns too fast)	1/4 cup	50 mL
Large onions, cut in wedges or chunks	3	3
Medium carrots, cut bite size	10	10
Sliced celery	1 1/2 cups	375 mL
Parsley flakes	1 tbsp.	15 mL
White wine (or alcohol-free wine)	1 cup	250 mL
Water	2 cups	500 mL
Beef bouillon cubes	3 x 1/5 oz.	3 × 6 g
Tomato sauce	2 x 7 1/2 oz.	2 × 213 mL
Lemon juice	1 tbsp.	15 mL

Combine flour, salt and pepper in plastic or paper bag. Shake well.

Add veal a few pieces at a time. Shake to coat.

Melt margarine in frying pan. Brown veal, adding more margarine if needed.

While shank pieces are browning, put onion, carrots, celery, and parsley in bottom of roaster. As meat is browned place over vegetables.

Pour wine into frying pan. Stir to loosen any bits of browned meat. Boil until reduced to about 1/4 original amount.

Add water and bouillon cubes. Stir to dissolve cubes.

Add tomato sauce and lemon juice. Mix together. Pour over contents in roaster. Cover. Cook in 325° F (160° C) oven for about 2 hours until meat is fork tender. Add more liquid if too dry. Gravy should be quite thick when meat is done. If it is too thin, remove meat to platter. Place vegetables over top. Keep warm. Boil sauce uncovered until it becomes a thick gravy. Serve gravy on the side. Serve with Risotto Milanese, page 104. Serves 8.

Pictured on page 107.

This is prepared in a very different way than other rice. A lot of stirring produces a good product. From Northern Italy.

Boiling water	8 cups	2 L
Chicken bouillon cubes, crumbled	8	8
Prepared chicken broth	1/2 cup	125 mL
Saffron, a pinch to make yellow		
Butter or margarine	1/2 cup	125 mL
Finely chopped onion	1 cup	250 mL
Long grain rice	2 cups	500 mL
Grated Parmesan cheese	1/2 cup	125 mL
Butter or margarine	2 tbsp.	30 mL
Grated Parmesan cheese, heavy sprinkle		

Boil water in large saucepan. Add bouillon cubes. Stir to dissolve. Keep hot.

Measure 1/2 cup (125 mL) chicken broth into small saucepan. Add saffron. Stir to dissolve.

Melt first amount of butter in large frying pan. Add onion. Sauté until lightly browned.

Add rice to onion. Stir constantly until a light gold color, about 10 to 15 minutes. Add 1 cup (250 mL) chicken broth. Stir until liquid is absorbed. Repeat 3 more times until a total of 4 cups (1 L) chicken broth has been added. Now add saffron-broth mixture. Stir until absorbed.

Add first amount of cheese. Stir. Continue to add chicken broth 1 cup (250 mL) at a time until rice is al-denté, tender but firm. Near the end of cooking time add broth in 1/2 cup (125 mL) additions. If rice is too dry after all broth has been used, add boiling water in 1/4 cup (50 mL) amounts. Total cooking and stirring time is about 30 to 35 minutes.

Add second amount of butter. Stir. Transfer to serving bowl. Sprinkle with grated Parmesan cheese. Serve with Osso Buco, page 103. Serves 8.

Pictured on page 107.

SWEET AND SOUR CARROTS

A very pleasant nip to this sauce.

Carrots, cut bite size	2¹/₂ lbs.	1.14 kg
Boiling salted water		
Butter or margarine	¹/₄ cup	50 mL
All-purpose flour	1 tbsp.	15 mL
Brown sugar	2 tbsp.	30 mL
Vinegar	2 tbsp.	30 mL
Salt	¹/₄ tsp.	1 mL
Pepper	¹/₈ tsp.	0.5 mL

Cook carrots in boiling salted water until tender. Drain and remove to bowl.

Melt butter in pot used to cook carrots. Mix in flour. Add sugar, vinegar, salt and pepper. Stir over medium heat until it boils and thickens. Add carrots. Heat and stir until hot and coated with sauce. Serves 8.

TOMATO SOLE

This is a snap to make. Assemble and put in the oven. Somewhat pepper-hot and so tasty.

Olive oil or cooking oil	3 tbsp.	50 mL
Garlic powder (or 1 clove, minced)	¹/₄ tsp.	1 mL
Cayenne pepper	¹/₄ tsp.	1 mL
Fillets of sole	4 lbs.	1.8 kg
Salt, sprinkle		
Pepper, sprinkle		
Canned tomatoes, cut up	1 cup	250 mL
White wine	¹/₄ cup	60 mL
Parsley for garnish		
Lemon wedges		

In large roaster heat olive oil, garlic powder and cayenne pepper together. A frying pan may be used for ¹/₂ recipe. Stir to mix.

Arrange fish in single layer, overlapping a bit if necessary. Sprinkle with salt and pepper. Spoon tomatoes over top. Drizzle wine all over. Cover. Bake in 400°F (200°C) oven for about 25 minutes until fish flakes when tested with a fork.

Serves 8.

MIXED SALAD

So fresh looking and appetizing. Greens are the main ingredient with ham, celery, cheese and tomatoes added.

Large head romaine lettuce	1	1
Tomatoes, halved, cut each half into 4 wedges	2	2
Sliced celery	1¹/₂ cups	375 mL
Provolone cheese or other mild smoked cheese, diced	¹/₂ cup	125 mL
Prosciutto or cooked ham, diced	¹/₂ cup	125 mL
Olive oil or cooking oil	¹/₄ cup	50 mL
Salt, sprinkle		
Red wine vinegar	1 tbsp.	15 mL
Lemon juice	1 tbsp.	15 mL

Tear lettuce into pieces and place in salad bowl. Add tomatoes, celery, cheese and prosciutto.

Pour olive oil over top. Toss to coat ingredients.

Sprinkle with salt and toss. Add vinegar and lemon juice. Toss again. Serves 8.

Italy

1. Tomato Cheese Salad page 100
2. Osso Buco page 103
3. Risotto Milanese page 104
4. Zabaglione page 113
5. Fried Mozzarella page 99
6. Stuffed Eggs page 98
7. Antipasto page 98
8. Cassata Alla Siciliana page 112

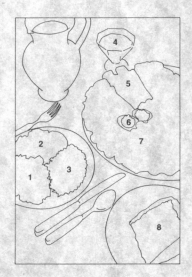

MEAT SAUCED SPAGHETTI

Served with a meaty sauce containing carrot and onion.

MEAT SAUCE

Ground beef	8 oz.	250 g
Grated carrot	1/2 cup	125 mL
Chopped onion	1/2 cup	125 mL
Olive oil, or cooking oil	2 tbsp.	30 mL
Canned tomatoes	19 oz.	540 mL
Granulated sugar	1 tsp.	5 mL
Oregano	1/2 tsp.	2 mL
Basil	1/2 tsp.	2 mL
Salt	1 tsp.	5 mL

PASTA

Spaghetti	1 lb.	454 g
Boiling water	4 qts.	5 L
Cooking oil	1 tbsp.	15 mL
Salt	1 tbsp.	15 mL
Butter or margarine	2 tbsp.	30 mL

Grated Parmesan cheese, heavy
  sprinkle

Meat Sauce: Cook ground beef, carrot and onion in olive oil in saucepan or frying pan until no pink remains in meat.

Add next 5 ingredients. Bring to a boil. Simmer 30 minutes uncovered until thick. Stir often. Makes 2 1/2 cups (575 mL).

Pasta: In large uncovered Dutch oven cook spaghetti in boiling water, cooking oil and salt until tender but firm. Drain. Return spaghetti to pot.

Add butter. Toss. Divide among eight 8 inch (20 cm) warm plates. Spoon meat sauce over top. Spaghetti may also be placed in center of large platter with meat sauce spooned around it.

Sprinkle with cheese. Serves 8 as a separate second course.

ZUCCHINI CASSEROLE

An excellent combination. Very good.

SAUCE

Butter or margarine	2 tbsp.	30 mL
Chopped onion	1 cup	250 mL
Finely chopped celery	1/2 cup	125 mL
Grated carrot	1/2 cup	125 mL
Canned tomatoes	14 oz.	398 mL
Tomato sauce	7 1/2 oz.	213 mL
Granulated sugar	1 tsp.	5 mL
Basil	1/2 tsp.	2 mL
Salt	1/2 tsp.	2 mL
Pepper	1/8 tsp.	0.5 mL

ZUCCHINI

Zucchini, medium size, unpeeled	8	8
Olive oil or cooking oil		
All-purpose flour	1 cup	250 mL
Eggs, beaten well	2	2

Grated Romano cheese, sprinkle

Sauce: Melt butter in frying pan. Add onion and celery. Sauté until soft.

Add remaining ingredients. Simmer uncovered until thick, about 20 to 25 minutes. Stir often.

Zucchini: Slice zucchini lengthwise into 1/2 inch (12 mm) thick slices.

Pour olive oil to 1/4 inch (6mm) depth in frying pan. Heat. Dip zucchini slices into flour then egg. Cook in olive oil, browning both sides well. They should be golden brown and fork tender.

In 3 quart (4 L) casserole layer sauce, zucchini, cheese sprinkle. Repeat until used up. Top 2 layers should be sauce and cheese. Bake uncovered in 350°F (180°C) oven for about 20 minutes until hot and browned. Serves 8.

EGGPLANT CASSEROLE: Make as for Zucchini Casserole substituting eggplant for zucchini.

The cheese in this rich tasting cake is ricotta and cottage cheese.
You would never guess.

CRUST

Butter or margarine	⅓ cup	75 mL
Graham cracker crumbs	1½ cups	350 mL
Granulated sugar	2 tbsp.	30 mL
Cocoa	2 tbsp.	30 mL

FILLING

Ricotta cheese, softened	1½ lbs.	700 g
Mascarpone cheese, softened (or cream cheese)	8 oz.	250 g
Granulated sugar	1 cup	250 mL
All-purpose flour	2 tbsp.	30 mL
Eggs	4	4
Vanilla	1½ tsp.	7 mL
Candied cut mixed fruit, chopped	3 tbsp.	50 mL
Semisweet chocolate baking squares, medium grated	2 × 1 oz.	2 × 28 g
Finely grated semisweet chocolate square	1 oz.	28 g

Crust: Melt butter in medium size saucepan over medium heat. Stir in crumbs, sugar and cocoa until mixed. Press into bottom of ungreased 9 inch (22 cm) springform pan. Bake in 350°F (180°C) oven for about 10 minutes.

Filling: Combine ricotta cheese, cream cheese, sugar and flour in mixing bowl. Beat until mixed.

Add eggs 1 at a time beating slowly after each addition. Add vanilla.

Stir in mixed fruit and first amount of grated chocolate. Turn into prepared pan. Bake in 350°F (180°C) oven for about 1 hour until set.

Sprinkle with grated chocolate. Chocolate will melt. Only part of the chocolate may be used if desired. Cool then chill.

Note: If ricotta cheese isn't available use cottage cheese. End result will be a bit softer.

CASSATA ALLA SICILIANA

A special cake very unique in flavor. Excellent.

CAKE

Eggs	3	3
Granulated sugar	1½ cups	375 mL
Vanilla	1 tsp.	5 mL
All-purpose flour	1½ cups	375 mL
Baking powder	1½ tsp.	7 mL
Salt	½ tsp.	2 mL
Butter or margarine	2 tbsp.	30 mL
Hot water	¾ cup	175 mL

Preheat oven to 350°F (180°C). Beat eggs in mixing bowl until well blended. Add sugar in 3 additions, beating well after each. Add vanilla.

Add flour, baking powder and salt. Stir to mix.

Melt butter in hot water in cup. Stir into batter. Pour into 2 greased 8 inch (20 cm) round layer pans. Bake for about 25 to 30 minutes until an inserted wooden pick comes out clean. Cool. Slice each layer in half to make a total of 4 layers.

RICOTTA FILLING

Ricotta cheese, room temperature	1 lb.	454 g
Granulated sugar	⅓ cup	75 mL
Milk	1 tbsp.	15 mL
Orange extract	1 tsp.	5 mL
Cut candied fruit, chopped	½ cup	125 mL
Semisweet chocolate chips, chopped	⅓ cup	75 mL

Break up ricotta cheese in mixing bowl. Add sugar, milk and orange extract. Beat until smooth. Add milk if needed for easy spreading.

Add fruit and chocolate chips. Mix. Spread between cake layers.

ICING

Semisweet chocolate chips	1 cup	250 mL
Water	3 tbsp.	50 mL
Orange extract	1 tsp.	5 mL
Butter or margarine	½ cup	125 mL
Icing (confectioner's) sugar	1½ cups	375 mL

Combine first 4 ingredients in saucepan over low heat. Stir often to hasten melting. When melted remove from heat.

Add icing sugar. Stir. Ice top and sides of cake. Icing will get firm fairly quickly.

Pictured on page 107.

A special light dessert.

Egg yolks	6	6
Granulated sugar	$^1/_3$ **cup**	75 mL
Marsala wine (or use sherry)	$^3/_4$ **cup**	175 mL

Combine egg yolks and sugar in top part of double boiler. Top of double boiler should hold at least 7 cups (1.6 L). With electric beater beat egg yolks and sugar until lemon colored and light. Add the wine. Mix. Place over simmering water. Be sure water in bottom pan doesn't touch top pan. Continue to beat mixture as t cooks and thickens. It will begin to get frothy and increase in volume. When it forms a soft mound it is done. Spoon into sherbets and serve warm or cold.

Makes 8 servings, $^1/_2$ cup (125 mL) each. Better to make recipe twice. If serving over fruit 1 recipe is enough.

Pictured on page 107.

He wondered about artificial respiration. He thought he'd rather have the real thing.

MEXICO

White sand beaches, sun, fun, mariachis, Aztec ruins, volcanoes, charros, tortillas, and refried beans are all familiar features of Mexico. Set your table and enjoy the smells and tastes of this fun-loving place!

Not all Mexican food is spicy. You can add as much or as little spice as you like. Experiment with chilies. To please everyone include a bowl of hot sauce and a bowl of mild sauce with your meal. Use white cheese such as Monterey Jack or Longhorn for an authentic Mexican look and taste.

Begin your meal with soup followed by rice and vegetables or spaghetti and tomato sauce. The next course could be red meat, fish or poultry accompanied by a salad or beans. A formal meal usually separates the beans from the meat course. The beans are served before dessert. Finish the meal with your choice of rice pudding, caramel flan or fresh fruit and chocolate.

Bien venido a Mexico!

MENU 1

*Corn Chili Soup   Page 116
Simple Rice   Page 124
*Chicken Enchiladas   Page 122
*Calabacitas   Page 131
Marinated Vegetable Salad   Page 118
*Refried Beans   Page 128
*Mexican Hot Sauce   Page 120
*Salsa Cruda   Page 117
Caramel Flan   Page 132
Coffee

MENU 2

*Tamale Pie   Page 115
Green Rice   Page 128
Chicken With Mole Sauce   Page 127
*Green Beans And Tomatoes   Page 129
Spinach Salad   Page 120
*Refried Beans   Page 128
*Mexican Hot Sauce   Page 120
*Salsa Cruda   Page 117
Rice Pudding   Page 133
Coffee

*Pictured page 125

MENU 3

Tortilla Soup   Page 116
Spaghetti   Page 130
Mexican Chorizos   Page 123 *or*
Red Snapper Veracruz Style   Page 121
Summer Squash   Page 130
Fruit Salad   Page 119
*Refried Beans   Page 128
*Mexican Hot Sauce   Page 120
*Salsa Cruda   Page 117
Mango Fluff   Page 132
Coffee

This is a real time saver, a lazy tamale. Meat filling sandwiched between layers of cornmeal batter.

FILLING

Cooking oil	1 tbsp.	15 mL
Ground beef	1 lb.	454 g
Chopped onion	1 cup	250 mL
Chopped green pepper	1/3 cup	75 mL
Garlic clove, minced	1	1
Canned tomatoes with juice, mashed	14 oz.	398 mL
Chili powder	1 tbsp.	15 mL
Salt	1 tsp.	5 mL
Pepper	1/4 tsp.	1 mL

CRUST

Cornmeal	2 cups	500 mL
Baking powder	1 tsp.	5 mL
Salt	1/2 tsp.	2 mL
Boiling water	5 1/4 cups	1.18 L

Filling: Heat cooking oil in frying pan. Add ground beef, onion, green pepper and garlic. Scramble-fry until browned.

Add next 4 ingredients. Bring to a boil. Simmer covered for 45 minutes.

Crust: Combine all 4 ingredients in large saucepan. Stir until it boils. Simmer gently uncovered for about 15 minutes until thick but still pourable. Pour 1/2 of this mixture into greased 8 x 8 inch (20 x 20 cm) pan. Spoon meat mixture over top. Cover with remaining crust. Bake in 350°F (180°C) oven for about 45 minutes until browned and firm. Serves 8 generously.

Pictured on page 125.

TORTILLA SOUP

This soup isn't complete without the tor-TEE-ah strips. They add lots of flavor.

Cooking oil	2 tbsp.	30 mL
Corn tortillas	5	5
Butter or margarine	1 tbsp.	15 mL
Chopped onion	³/₄ cup	175 mL
Water	8 cups	2 L
Cooked chicken, shredded	2¹/₂ cups	625 mL
Canned chopped green chilies	4 oz.	114 mL
Chicken bouillon powder	3 tbsp.	50 mL
Parsley flakes	¹/₂ tsp.	2 mL
Salt	¹/₂ tsp.	2 mL

Heat cooking oil until hot. Cut tortillas into ¹/₂ inch (12 mm) strips. Cut each strip in 2 or 3 pieces. Fry in hot cooking oil until crisp and browned. Drain on paper towels.

Heat butter and onion in large saucepan over medium heat. Sauté onion until clear and soft.

Add remaining ingredients. Bring to a boil, stirring often. Simmer slowly, covered, for about 15 minutes. Ladle into 8 soup bowls. Add tortilla strips. Serves 8 people about 1 cup (250 mL) each.

CORN CHILI SOUP

Delicious soup with just the right amount of mild chili flavor.

Butter or margarine	2 tbsp.	30 mL
Chopped onion	¹/₄ cup	60 mL
All-purpose flour	2 tbsp.	30 mL
Salt	1 tsp.	5 mL
Pepper	¹/₄ tsp.	1 mL
Milk	4 ¹/₃ cups	1 L
Chicken bouillon cubes	2 × ¹/₅ oz.	2 × 6 g
Boiling water	1 cup	250 mL
Cream style corn, smoothed in blender	2 × 14 oz.	2 × 398 mL
Canned chopped green chilies	3 tbsp.	50 mL

(continued on next page)

Sour cream	1/2 cup	125 mL
Chopped green onions	1/4 cup	60 mL

Melt butter in large saucepan. Add onion. Sauté until soft.

Mix in flour, salt and pepper. Stir in milk until t boils and thickens.

Dissolve bouillon cubes in boiling water. Add to saucepan.

Stir in corn and chilies. Heat thoroughly. Pour into 8 soup bowls.

Mix sour cream and green onion together. Divide over top of soup in bowls. Serves 8 people 1 cup (225 mL) each

Note: Kernel corn may be smoothed in blender instead of using cream style. Use about 3 1/2 to 4 cups (800 to 900 mL).

Pictured on page 125.

SALSA CRUDA

SAHL-sah CROO-dah is used regularly for dipping and saucing.

Tomatoes, diced	2	2
Canned chopped green chilies, drained, finely chopped	4 oz.	114 mL
Dry onion flakes	2 tsp.	10 mL
Parsley flakes	1 tsp.	5 mL
Granulated sugar	1/2 tsp.	2 mL
Garlic powder	1/8 tsp.	0.5 mL
Salt, sprinkle		
Pepper, sprinkle		
Lemon juice	1/2 tsp.	2 mL

Combine all 9 ingredients in bowl. Stir together. Chill for 1 1/2 to 2 hours before serving. Use like ketchup for meat balls. Also use as a dip for tortilla chips. Makes about 1 1/3 cups (300 mL).

Pictured on page 125.

MARINATED VEGETABLE SALAD

To obtain the more authentic zing to this dish simply omit the water when making the brine. Lots of color in this.

Small onion cut in very thin rings	1	1
Cold water to cover		
Cauliflower florets, cooked tender-crisp	$^3/_4$ cup	175 mL
Sliced carrot, cooked tender-crisp	$^1/_2$ cup	125 mL
Thinly sliced celery	$^1/_2$ cup	125 mL
Short zucchini fingers	$^1/_2$ cup	125 mL
Red pepper, cut matchstick size	$^1/_2$ cup	125 mL
BRINE		
Water	1 cup	250 mL
Vinegar	1 cup	250 mL
Canned chopped green chilies	4 oz.	114 mL
Salt	$^1/_2$ tsp.	2 mL
Pepper	$^1/_8$ tsp.	0.5 mL
Oregano	$^1/_2$ tsp.	2 mL
Garlic powder	$^1/_2$ tsp.	2 mL

Put onion rings in cold water. Let stand 1 hour. Drain.

Combine next 5 ingredients in bowl. Add onion.

Brine: In saucepan combine all 7 ingredients. Bring to a boil over medium heat. Simmer for 10 minutes. Pour over vegetables. Cool then chill for two days before serving. Serves 8.

Paré Pointer

If you stay up all night wondering where the sun went, it will finally dawn on you.

A very fresh and colorful salad.

DRESSING

Avocado, peeled, pitted and mashed	1	1
Mayonnaise	²/₃ cup	150 mL
Lemon juice	1 tbsp.	15 mL
Granulated sugar	1 tbsp.	15 mL

SALAD

Lettuce leaves	6	6
Pink grapefruit, peeled, cut in bite size pieces	1	1
Papaya, peeled, cut in bite size pieces	1	1
Oranges, peeled, cut in bite size pieces	2	2
Canned pineapple chunks, drained, reserve juice	14 oz.	398 mL
Cooking apples, peeled and diced	1	1
Bananas, peeled and sliced	2	2
Reserved pineapple juice		
Pomegranate, seeds only	1	1

Dressing: Mix all 4 ingredients together. Chill until needed.

Salad: Line glass bowl with lettuce leaves.

In another bowl combine next 4 ingredients. Toss.

Combine apple, banana and juice in small bowl. Toss to coat. Drain well. Add to rest of fruit. Toss. Turn into prepared bowl.

Sprinkle with some pomegranate seeds. Serve with dressing on the side. Put rest of seeds in a separate dish. Serves 8 generously.

SPINACH SALAD

Different and refreshing.

Large bunch of spinach leaves	1	1
Pink grapefruit, peeled and cut in bite size pieces	1	1
Canned chick peas, drained (or use dried, cooked)	1 cup	250 mL
Zucchini, 7 inch (18 cm), unpeeled, cut matchstick size	1	1
LIME DRESSING		
Salad dressing (such as Miracle Whip)	¼ cup	60 mL
Lime juice	1 tbsp.	15 mL
Granulated sugar	1 tbsp.	15 mL
Pine nuts	3 tbsp.	50 mL

Tear spinach leaves or leave whole and place into bowl . Add grapefruit, chick peas and zucchini.

Lime Dressing: Mix salad dressing, lime juice and sugar together in bowl. Stir. Pour over salad and toss.

Add pine nuts. Toss again. Serves 8.

MEXICAN HOT SAUCE

For an authentic taste you will want to add more dried red chilies.

Medium tomatoes, peeled and diced	3	3
Finely chopped onion	⅓ cup	75 mL
Chopped chives	1 tbsp.	15 mL
Parsley flakes	1 tsp.	5 mL
Dried red chilies or crushed red pepper	½ tsp.	2 mL
Salt, light sprinkle		
Granulated sugar	¼ tsp.	1 mL

Measure all ingredients into bowl. Stir to mix. Make at least 30 minutes before serving so flavors can blend. Makes about 1 cup (250 mL).

Pictured on page 125.

A great make ahead dish. When ready just pour sauce over fish and bake.

Butter or margarine	2 tbsp.	30 mL
Chopped onion	1 cup	250 mL
Garlic clove, minced	1	1
Canned tomatoes	14 oz.	398 mL
Green pimiento-stuffed olives	1/2 cup	125 mL
Capers (optional)	2 tbsp.	30 mL
Bay leaf	1	1
Salt	1 tsp.	5 mL
Pepper	1/4 tsp.	1 mL
Red snapper fillets	3 lbs.	1.36 kg
Lemon or lime wedges		

Melt butter in large saucepan over medium heat. Add onion and garlic. Sauté until soft but not browned.

Add next 6 ingredients. Bring to a boil. Simmer slowly uncovered for about 10 minutes. Discard bay leaf.

Cut fillets into serving size pieces. Arrange in small greased roaster. Pour sauce over fish. Cover. Bake in 350°F (180°C) oven for about 25 to 30 minutes until it flakes when tested with fork.

Serve with lemon wedges. Serves 8.

Archeologists don't have much help when they find dinosaur bones. They work with a skeleton crew.

Shredded chicken combined with cheese and rolled into bundles then topped and baked with a tomato and green chili sauce. Allow extra time to prepare. To be authentic use Monterey Jack cheese or other white cheese.

Chicken breasts (about 2)	1½ lbs.	640 g
Chicken thighs (about 6)	1¾ lbs.	825 g
Onion, chopped	½ cup	125 mL
Celery, sliced	¼ cup	50 mL
Bay leaf	1	1
Salt	2 tsp.	10 mL
Pepper	½ tsp.	2 mL
Water to cover		

FILLING

Butter or margarine	2 tbsp.	30 mL
Chopped onion	1 cup	250 mL
Grated Monterey Jack cheese	1½ cups	375 mL
Grated Parmesan cheese	⅓ cup	75 mL
Cooking oil	½ cup	125 mL
Corn tortillas	16	16

SAUCE

Condensed cream of chicken soup	10 oz.	284 mL
Canned tomatoes, drained	28 oz.	796 mL
Canned chopped green chilies	2 × 4 oz.	2 × 114 mL
Sour cream	½ cup	125 mL
Granulated sugar	1 tsp.	5 mL
Garlic powder	¼ tsp.	1 mL
Onion powder	¼ tsp.	1 mL
Grated Cheddar cheese (or white cheese)	2 cups	500 mL

GARNISH

Sour cream	1 cup	250 mL
Sliced green onion	2 tbsp.	30 mL
Black olives and avocado slices (optional)		

(continued on next page)

Combine first 8 ingredients in large Dutch oven. Boil until chicken is tender, about 30 to 40 minutes. Cool chicken in broth. Measure and reserve 2 cups (500 mL) broth. Remove chicken meat from bones and shred. You should have about 4 cups (1 L).

Filling: Heat butter in frying pan. Add onion. Sauté until soft. Cool.

Measure Monterey Jack cheese and Parmesan cheese into bowl. Add onion and chicken. Toss to mix.

Heat cooking oil in frying pan. Using tongs dip tortilla into cooking oil to soften for 3 to 5 seconds per side adding more oil if needed. Drain on paper towels. Place scant ¼ cup (60 mL) chicken mixture on tortilla. Press filling together. Roll tortilla tightly around chicken. Place in 1 or 2 greased pans in single layer seam side down.

Sauce: In bowl mix first 7 ingredients together. Pour over enchiladas.

Sprinkle cheese over top. Bake in 350°F (180°C) oven until bubbly hot, about 25 minutes.

Garnish: Place 2 enchiladas close together on each plate. Spoon 2 tbsp. (30 mL) sour cream over the middle of both. Sprinkle 1 tsp. (5 mL) sliced green onion over sour cream. Add an avocado slice and black olives if desired. Makes about 18 Serves 8.

Pictured on page 125.

MEXICAN CHORIZO

A tasty, easy to make sausage meat.

Ground pork	**3 lbs.**	**1.36 kg**
Vinegar	**⅓ cup**	**75 mL**
Chili powder	**2 tbsp.**	**30 mL**
Salt	**1 tbsp.**	**15 mL**
Pepper	**½ tsp.**	**2 mL**
Oregano	**2 tsp.**	**10 mL**
Garlic powder	**½ tsp.**	**2 mL**

Put ground pork into bowl.

Combine next 6 ingredients in separate small bowl. Mix well, adding water to mix if too dry. Add to pork. Mix thoroughly. Let stand in refrigerator at least 1 day for flavors to blend. Divide into 4 equal balls. Divide each ball into 4 patties. Fry, browning both sides, until no pink remains. Makes 16 patties. Serves 8 people 2 patties each.

A variation of rice that is much used and enjoyed.

Long grain rice	2 cups	500 mL
Hot water to cover		
Cooking oil	¼ cup	60 mL
Medium tomatoes	2	2
Chopped onion	½ cup	125 mL
Water	4 cups	1 L
Salt	1 tsp.	5 mL
Chicken bouillon powder	2 tsp.	10 mL

Measure rice into bowl. Cover with very hot water and let stand for 15 minutes. Drain. Cover with cold water. Drain. Repeat cold water rinse until water runs clear when draining.

Put drained rice and cooking oil into cold frying pan. Heat. Sauté stirring often until browned, about 10 minutes.

Combine remaining ingredients in blender. Blend until smooth. Pour into saucepan and heat. Add rice. It will spatter quite a bit. Bring to a boil. Cover. Simmer slowly until water is absorbed, about 15 minutes. Fluff with fork. Taste for salt adding more if desired. Serves 8.

Mexico

1. Mexican Hot Sauce page 120
2. Salsa Cruda page 117
3. Tamale Pie page 115
4. Corn Chili Soup page 116
5. Calabacitas page 131
6. Chicken Enchiladas page 122
7. Refried Beans page 128

A good Mexican dish. Spicy hot moh-LAY sauce contains chocolate.

Chicken parts (whole chicken may be cut up)	6 lbs.	2.7 kg
Salt	1 tsp.	5 mL
Medium onion, quartered	1	1
Water to cover		
Large green pepper, chopped	1	1
Chopped onion	1/2 cup	125 mL
Garlic cloves, halved	2	2
Canned tomatoes	14 oz.	398 mL
Raisins	1/3 cup	75 mL
Blanched almonds	1/4 cup	60 mL
Toasted sesame seeds	2 tbsp.	30 mL
Cinnamon	1/4 tsp.	1 mL
Cloves	1/8 tsp.	0.5 mL
Bread slices, toasted and dried, broken in pieces	2	2
Semisweet baking chocolate square	1/2 x 1 oz.	1/2 x 28 g
Lard or cooking oil	2 tbsp.	30 mL
All-purpose flour	1/4 cup	60 mL
Dried crushed chilies	1 tbsp.	15 mL
Salt	1 tsp.	5 mL
Pepper	1/4 tsp.	1 mL
Reserved chicken broth	4 cups	1 L
Toasted sesame seeds	2 tbsp.	30 mL

Place chicken, first amount of salt and onion in large Dutch oven. Cover with water. Bring to a boil. Cook covered until chicken is tender, about 1 hour. Drain. Reserve broth.

Measure next 11 ingredients into blender or food processor. Blend smooth.

Melt lard in large saucepan over medium heat. Mix in flour, chilies, and second amount of salt and pepper. Stir in reserved broth until it boils and thickens. Add blender contents. Stir. Add chicken pieces. Simmer to heat through.

To serve, sprinkle with remaining sesame seeds. Serves 8.

REFRIED BEANS

Pinto beans make the lightest colored product followed by red beans and then black beans. A must for a Mexican meal.

Dry beans, pinto, red or black	2 cups	500 mL
Hot water to cover		
Chopped onion	1 cup	250 mL
Bay leaf	1	1
Salt	1 tsp.	5 mL
Garlic powder	1/4 tsp.	1 mL
Bacon slices, diced	6	6
Bacon drippings, lard or cooking oil	1/4 cup	50 mL
Pepper, sprinkle (optional)		
Grated Monterey Jack cheese for garnish		

Measure first 7 ingredients into large heavy saucepan. Bring to a boil. Simmer covered until tender, about 1 hour 45 minutes. Add more water as needed but not too much near the end of cooking as liquid isn't needed when beans are cooked. Discard bay leaf. Mash beans leaving up to 1/4 of them only partially mashed. This can be done while beans are hot or cold.

Melt drippings in frying pan. Add beans. Heat. Stir often. If serving separately, divide among 8 plates. Sprinkle with grated cheese. Makes about 5 cups.

Variation: Stir about 3/4 cup (175 mL) grated Monterey Jack cheese into hot beans before serving.

Pictured on page 125.

GREEN RICE

Delicate green in color this makes a good variation.

Long grain rice	2 cups	500 mL
Hot water to cover		
Large green peppers, seeded, cut up	3	3
Chopped onion	1 cup	250 mL
Parsley flakes	1/3 cup	75 mL

(continued on next page)

Garlic clove	1	1
Chicken bouillon cubes	4 x ¹/₅ oz.	4 × 6 g
Water	1 cup	250 mL
Salt	1 tsp.	5 mL
Pepper	¹/₈ tsp.	0.5 mL
Cooking oil	3 tbsp.	50 mL
Water	3 cups	750 mL

Cover rice in bowl with very hot water. Let stand 15 minutes. Drain. Pour cold water over rice to cover. Drain. Continue to rinse with cold water until water runs clear when draining.

Measure next 8 ingredients into blender. Blend until smooth. Set aside.

Put cooking oil into large saucepan. Add rice to cold saucepan so it won't spatter. Place over medium heat. Fry, stirring often, until rice is golden brown. Add contents of blender.

Add remaining water. Bring to a boil. Simmer slowly, covered, until tender and liquid is absorbed, about 15 minutes. Fluff with fork. Serves 8.

GREEN BEANS AND TOMATOES

Colorful, good and so easy to prepare.

Bacon slices, diced	6	6
Chopped onion	1 cup	250 mL
Canned tomatoes	1 cup	250 mL
Canned cut green beans, drained	2 x 14 oz.	2 x 398 mL

Sauté bacon and onion in frying pan until cooked.

Heat tomatoes and green beans in saucepan. Add bacon and onion. Serves 8.

SPAGHETTI

Served in Mexico often as an alternative to rice. This heats in the oven. A smooth red pepper sauce and melting chunks of cheese.

Spaghetti	1 lb.	454 g
Boiling water	5 qts.	6 L
Cooking oil	2 tbsp.	30 mL
Salt	4 tsp.	20 mL
Light cream	1 cup	250 mL
Large red pepper, seeded, **cut up**	1	1
Diced Monterey Jack cheese	2 cups	500 mL

In uncovered Dutch oven cook spaghetti in boiling water, cooking oil and salt until tender but firm, about 11 to 13 minutes. Drain. Return spaghetti to pot.

Put cream and red pepper into blender. Blend until smooth. Pour into small saucepan. Heat but don't boil. Pour over spaghetti.

Add cheese. Toss. Turn into 3 quart (3.5 L) greased casserole. Bake covered in 350°F (180°C) oven until bubbling hot, about 25 minutes. Serves 8.

SUMMER SQUASH

Parmesan cheese, green chilies and onion add flavor to zucchini.

Chopped onion	1 cup	250 mL
Cooking oil	¹/₄ cup	50 mL

Zucchini or yellow squash
   about 6 inches (15 cm)
   long cut into small cubes
	6	6

Canned diced green chilies	4 oz.	114 mL
Milk	¹/₃ cup	75 mL
Salt	¹/₂ tsp.	2 mL
Pepper	¹/₄ tsp.	1 mL
Grated Parmesan cheese	¹/₃ cup	75 mL

(continued on next page)

Sauté onion in cooking oil in frying pan for 3 to 4 minutes.

Add zucchini. Cook about 5 minutes longer until tender.

Add green chilies, milk, salt and pepper. Heat through. Turn into serving bowl.

Add cheese. Toss to mix. Serves 8.

CALABACITAS

This cah-lah-bah-SEE-tas contains zucchini, corn. tomato sauce and onion. The word means little squash.

Cooking oil	2 tbsp.	30 mL
Chopped onion	1 cup	250 mL
Garlic clove, minced	1	1
Zucchini, about 6 inches (15 cm) long, unpeeled, sliced	4-5	4-5
Kernel corn, fresh or frozen	1¹/₂ cups	325 mL
Tomato sauce	7¹/₂ oz.	213 mL
Canned chopped green chilies	4 oz.	114 mL
Granulated sugar	¹/₂ tsp.	2 mL
Salt	1 tsp.	5 mL
Pepper	¹/₃ tsp.	0.5 mL
Grated Monterey Jack cheese	¹/₂ cup	125 mL

Heat cooking oil in large frying pan. Add onion and garlic. Sauté for about 3 minutes.

Add zucchini and corn. Stir and cook for 3 or 4 minutes until tender.

Add next 5 ingredients. Heat until bubbling. Pour into bowl.

Sprinkle with cheese. Serves 8.

Pictured on page 125.

MANGO FLUFF

And a light bit of fluff it is. A milky peach color.

Cold water	½ cup	125 mL
Unflavored gelatin powders	2 × ¼ oz.	2 × 7 g
Granulated sugar	¾ cup	175 mL
Lemon juice	2 tbsp.	30 mL
Salt	⅛ tsp.	0.5 mL
Mashed mango (or papaya)	2 cups	500 mL
Rum flavoring	½ tsp.	2 mL
Vanilla flavoring	¼ tsp.	1 mL
Whipping cream (or 2 envelopes topping)	2 cups	500 mL
Rum flavoring	¼ tsp.	1 mL
Slivered or flaked almonds	2 tbsp.	30 mL

Measure cold water into saucepan. Sprinkle gelatin over top. Let stand for 5 minutes. Place over medium heat. Stir to dissolve gelatin.

Add sugar, lemon juice and salt. Stir until sugar is dissolved. Remove from heat.

Add mango, first amount of rum flavoring and vanilla flavoring. Mix well. Chill until mixture will hold its shape when spoonful taken from one side of mixture is placed over top of other side.

Beat cream until stiff. Measure and reserve 1 cup (250 mL) keeping it chilled. Fold the rest of the whipped cream into thickened mango mixture. Scoop into pretty bowl. Chill.

Stir in second amount of rum flavoring to reserved whipped cream. Spread over center or around outside edge of bowl. Sprinkle with almonds. Serves 8.

CARAMEL FLAN

A different custard with condensed milk for flavor and a yummy caramel topping.

Granulated sugar	¾ cup	175 mL
Eggs	5	5

(continued on next page)

Sweetened condensed milk	11 oz.	300 mL
Evaporated milk	14 oz.	385 mL
Vanilla	1 tsp.	5 mL

Heat sugar in heavy frying pan over medium heat until melted and dark brown in color. Stir often. Pour into 8 or 9 inch (20 or 22 cm) round casserole. Tilt dish to coat sides.

Beat eggs and condensed milk in mixing bowl. Add evaporated milk and vanilla. Beat slowly to mix. Pour into prepared dish. Set in pan containing hot water. Bake in 350°F (180°C) oven until an inserted knife comes out clean, about 1 hour. Cool then chill for several hours or overnight. Run a knife around outside edge. Put large plate over top. Invert quickly. Custard will now be on the bottom with caramel on top and around the sides. Cut into 8 wedges for 8 medium servings.

RICE PUDDING

This just might be the best rice pudding you will ever eat.

Long grain rice	1 cup	250 mL
Water	2 cups	500 mL
Cinnamon stick (about 4 inch, 10 cm)	1	1
Milk	4 cups	1 L
Granulated sugar	1 cup	250 mL
Raisins	1/2 cup	125 mL
Salt	1/4 tsp.	1 mL
Egg yolks	3	3
Vanilla	1 tsp.	5 mL

Combine rice, water and cinnamon stick in medium saucepan. Cover and bring to a boil. Simmer until rice is cooked and all the water is absorbed, about 15 minutes. Remove cinnamon stick.

Heat milk in heavy saucepan. Stir in sugar, raisins and salt. Add rice. Simmer slowly uncovered until thick but still soft, about 15 minutes. Stir often.

Beat egg yolks in small bowl. Stir in vanilla. Add about 1/2 cup (125 mL) hot rice to egg yolk mixture. Stir all of this back into hot rice. Cook and stir for about 1 minute. Ready to serve 8 people 3/4 cup (175 mL) each.

UNITED STATES OF AMERICA

An exciting venture into this fantastic and colorful country takes you from New York with the Statue of Liberty to Hollywood and its stars, onto New Orleans and the Mardi Gras, then to Disneyland with everything for a child's imagination.

People the world over contributed to the cuisine of this country. To some extent, cooking in the United States has evolved into a national flavor, but some regional distinctions are obvious. Neighoring influence and that of new people to the country are bound to have an effect. California cuisine is one example, with a lot of oriental and Mexican influence. A delightful and zesty difference can be tasted in the Cajun cooking of Louisiana, see Menu 1. The New England states also lay claim to some distinct regional flavors, including seafood.

They always tell you one thing about dinner in the U.S.A....Y'all come back for more!

MENU 1

*Hurricane Page 135
*Gumbo Page 136
*Creole Dressed Salad Page 138
*Jambalya Page 140
*Creamed Spinach Page 147
*Bread Pudding Page 148
*Whiskey Sauce Page 148
Coffee   Tea

MENU 2

Clam Chowder Page 137
Pacific Rim Salad Page 138 *or*
Crunchy Salad Page 139
Baked Pork Chops Page 142 *or*
Kentucky Hot Brown Page 146 *or*
Corned Beef and Cabbage Page135
Zippy Sauce Page 137
Baby Jacket Potatoes Page 141
Sweet Potato Praline Page 141 *or*
Scalloped Mushrooms Page 145
Derby Pie Page 149 *or*
Boston Cream Pie Page 150
Coffee   Tea

*Pictured page 143

HURRICANE

No dinner party from New Orleans is complete without a hurricane. Good with or without alcohol.

Raspberry flavored drink	3 cups	750 mL
Passion fruit juice (or fruit blend)	2 cups	500 mL
Lime juice	4 tsp.	20 mL
Citric acid	¼ tsp.	1 mL
Crushed ice (or cubes)		
Rum		
Orange wedges for garnish		
Maraschino cherries for garnish		

Combine first 4 ingredients in pitcher. Chill

Fill glass with crushed ice. An authentic hurricane glass holds 28 oz. (795 mL). However, your regular glasses will do nicely. Pour a portion of rum over ice. Fill glass with raspberry mix.

Garnish with orange and cherry. Makes 5 cups (1.25 L) hurricane mix.

CORNED BEEF AND CABBAGE

Sit down to a New England dinner from the north-eastern states. For small quantities vegetables are added to and cooked with the meat.

Corned beef brisket	4 lbs.	1.8 kg
Water to cover		
Medium potatoes, quartered	8	8
Boiling salted water		
Head of cabbage, 1½ lbs. (700 g)	1	1
Turnip, cut in cubes	2 lbs.	1 kg

Put corned beef into Dutch oven. Add first amount of water. Cover and boil for about 3 hours until tender. Remove meat to another container and keep hot. Reserve corned beef water.

Add potatoes to corned beef water. Cut cabbage in half. Cut each half into 4 wedges and add to potatoes. Add turnip. Boil until vegetables are tender. Dish up vegetables and meat onto warm platter and bowls. Serve with Zippy Sauce, page 137. Serves 8.

A very full soup. Only small portions are served as a first course. Soup is ladled over a scoop of rice in each bowl.

Cooking oil	2 tbsp.	30 mL
Spicy-hot sausage, cut up	1 lb.	454 g
Chicken thighs, boned, cut up	1¹/₂ lbs.	700 g
All-purpose flour	¹/₂ cup	125 mL
Cooking oil	¹/₂ cup	125 mL
Water	4 cups	1 L
Chopped onion	2 cups	500 mL
Chopped celery	¹/₂ cup	125 mL
Chopped green pepper	¹/₂ cup	125 mL
Canned sliced okra with juice	14 oz.	398 mL
Garlic clove, minced	1	1
Chicken bouillon powder	1¹/₂ tbsp.	25 mL
Salt	1 tsp.	5 mL
Cayenne pepper	¹/₈ tsp.	0.5 mL
Long grain rice	²/₃ cup	150 mL
Boiling water	1¹/₃ cups	300 mL
Salt	¹/₂ tsp.	2 mL

In large frying pan heat first amount of cooking oil over medium heat. Add sausage and chicken. Cook, stirring often until done. Using slotted spoon, remove meat to bowl.

Measure flour and second amount of cooking oil into clean frying pan. This is a roux. Stir until roux turns to a dark tan color. Don't scorch it. Stir continually.

When desired color is reached transfer mixture to large saucepan. Add next 9 ingredients and stir. Add meat. Bring to a boil. Cover and simmer slowly for about 50 minutes.

Meanwhile cook rice in boiling water and salt at a slow simmer in covered saucepan for about 15 minutes. Serve one scoop of rice into each bowl. Pour soup over top. Serves 8.

Pictured on page 143.

New England clam chowder is known everywhere. Always eaten with relish.

Diced potatoes	3 cups	700 mL
Water	1½ cups	375 mL
Salt	1 tsp.	5 mL
Butter or margarine	2 tbsp.	30 mL
Chopped onion	1½ cup	375 mL
Bacon slices, diced	4	4
Chopped celery	½ cup	125 mL
Milk	4 cups	900 mL
Pepper	½ tsp.	2 mL
Canned minced baby clams with juice	10 oz.	284 mL

Cook potatoes in salted water until tender. Cook slowly and keep covered so water will not evaporate. Do not drain.

Melt butter in frying pan . Add onion, bacon and celery. Sauté until onion is soft and clear.

Mix in flour and pepper. Stir in milk until it boils and thickens.

Add clams with juice. Heat through. Serves 8 people 1 cup (225 mL) each.

The perfect sauce to serve with corned beef.

Butter or margarine	⅓ cup	75 mL
All-purpose flour	⅓ cup	75 mL
Milk	4 cups	900 mL
Salt	1 tsp.	5 mL
Pepper	¼ tsp.	1 mL
Parsley flakes	½ tsp.	2 mL
Horseradish	2 tsp.	10 mL
Prepared mustard	1½ tsp.	2 mL

Melt butter in medium saucepan. Mix in flour. Add remaining ingredients. Stir until it boils and thickens. Serve with corned beef meal. Makes about 3½ cups (800 mL).

PACIFIC RIM SALAD

Great mixture. Great flavor. Great color.

Chopped lettuce, lightly packed	4 cups	1 L
Fresh bean sprouts	1 cup	250 mL
Cooked chicken, cut bite size	1 cup	250 mL
Short slivers red pepper	1/4 cup	50 mL
Short slivers yellow pepper	1/4 cup	50 mL
Short slivers green pepper	1/4 cup	50 mL
Sliced water chestnuts	1/4 cup	50 mL
Short slivers carrot	1/4 cup	50 mL
Chopped green onion	2 tbsp.	30 mL
Cooking oil	2 tbsp.	30 mL
Wonton wrappers	8	8
Sliced almonds, toasted	1/4 cup	50 mL
HOISIN DRESSING		
Hoisin sauce	1/4 cup	50 mL
Cooking oil	1 tbsp.	15 mL
Vinegar	1 tbsp.	15 mL

Combine first 9 ingredients in large bowl.

Heat cooking oil until hot. Cut wonton wrappers into 1/2 inch (12 mm) strips. Cut each strip into 2 pieces. Fry in hot cooking oil until crisp and browned. Drain on paper towels.

Add almonds to wonton wrapper strips.

Hoisin Dressing: Mix all 3 ingredients together in small bowl. When ready to serve pour dressing over salad in large bowl. Add wonton wrappers and almonds. Toss. Serves 8.

CREOLE DRESSED SALAD

A bit of a nip to this dressed salad. Very good.

Large head of Romaine lettuce, torn	1	1
Croutons	1 cup	250 mL
Grated Parmesan cheese	1/3 cup	75 mL

(continued on next page)

CREOLE DRESSING

Butter or margarine	2 tbsp.	30 mL
Chopped onion	2/3 cup	150 mL
Chopped green pepper	1/2 cup	125 mL
Canned tomatoes, drained	1/3 cup	75 mL
Granulated sugar	1 tsp.	5 mL
Salt	1 tsp.	5 mL
Pepper	1/4 tsp.	1 mL
Hot pepper sauce	1/4 tsp.	1 mL
Mayonnaise	1/2 cup	125 mL

Put lettuce, croutons and cheese into large bowl.

Creole Dressing: Melt butter in frying pan. Add onion and green pepper. Sauté until soft. Cool.

Beat tomatoes, sugar, salt and pepper together in small bowl. Mix in hot pepper sauce and mayonnaise. Stir into onion mixture. Pour about 2/3 of this over lettuce. Toss. Add more dressing if needed. Serves 8.

Pictured on page 143

CRUNCHY SALAD

Very flavorful. Crunchy good.

Bite size pieces of cauliflower	4 cups	1 L
Bite size pieces of broccoli	4 cups	1 L
Medium red onion, slivered	2	2
Bacon slices, crispy fried and crumbled	10	10

DRESSING		
Salad dressing (such as Miracle Whip)	1 1/2 cups	375 mL
Prepared mustard	1 1/2 tbsp.	25 mL
Granulated sugar	1 1/2 tbsp.	25 mL
Vinegar	2 tbsp.	30 mL

Combine first 4 ingredients in large bowl.

Dressing: Mix all 4 ingredients together. Pour over vegetables. Toss until vegetables are coated. Turn into serving bowl. Serves 8.

# JAMBALAYA

A traditional favorite in the southern state of Louisiana. Contains rice, meat and some vegetables.

Cooking oil	3 tbsp.	50 mL
Chicken parts, skin removed	4 lbs.	1.8 kg
Salt, good sprinkle		
Pepper, good sprinkle		
Smoked hot sausage or smoked ham, cut up	2 lbs.	900 g
Chopped onion	2$\frac{1}{2}$ cups	625 mL
Chopped celery	1 cup	250 mL
Chopped green pepper	1 cup	250 mL
Garlic clove, minced	1	1
Boiling water	3 cups	750 mL
Chicken bouillon cubes	3 $\times$ $\frac{1}{5}$ oz.	3 $\times$ 6 g
Long grain rice	2$\frac{1}{3}$ cups	575 mL
Cayenne pepper	$\frac{1}{4}$ tsp.	1 mL
Salt	$\frac{1}{2}$ tsp.	2 mL

Heat cooking oil in frying pan. Brown chicken. Sprinkle with salt and pepper. Transfer to tray.

Brown sausage adding more cooking oil if necessary. Transfer to tray.

Combine onion, celery, green pepper and garlic in frying pan. Add more cooking oil if needed. Sauté until tender. Remove from heat.

Put boiling water and bouillon cubes into large pot over medium heat. Stir to dissolve cubes.

Add rice, cayenne pepper and salt to water. Add chicken, sausage and onion mixture. Stir lightly. Cover. Simmer to cook rice about 15 minutes. Taste for salt, pepper and cayenne. Serves 8.

Pictured on page 143.

BABY JACKET POTATOES

These tiny new potatoes will tend to dominate the meal.

Small new potatoes	**3 lbs.**	**1.36 kg**
Boiling salted water		
Butter or margarine	**6 tbsp.**	**100 mL**
Granulated sugar	**4 tbsp.**	**60 mL**

Cook washed new potatoes with skin intact in boiling salted water until tender. Drain.

Heat butter and sugar in frying pan until light y browned. Add potatoes a few at a time turning to coat each potato w th mixture. Serves 8.

SWEET POTATO PRALINE

This delectable recipe originates from the deep south and New Orleans. It is so good you can pretend ycu're eating dessert.

Sweet potatoes	**2¹/₂ lbs.**	**1.13 kg**
Boiling salted water		
Butter or margarine	**¹/₄ cup**	**50 mL**
Granulated sugar	**1 tbsp.**	**15 mL**
Egg, beaten	**1**	**1**
Vanilla	**¹/₂ tsp.**	**2 mL**
TOPPING		
Brown sugar, packed	**1 cup**	**250 mL**
Whipping cream	**¹/₂ cup**	**125 mL**
Butter or margarine	**¹/₄ cup**	**50 mL**
Chopped pecans	**³/₄ cup**	**175 mL**

Peel potatoes and cut in chunks. Cook in salted water until tender. Drain well. Mash. You should have about 4 cups (1 L).

Add butter, sugar, egg and vanilla. Mash well. Pack in 3 quart (4L) casserole. Set aside.

Topping: In small heavy saucepan combine brown sugar and cream. Stir. Bring to a boil over medium heat. Cook until soft-ball stage is reached on candy thermometer or until a teaspoonful dropped in very cold water forms a soft ball. Remove from heat.

Stir in butter and pecans. Spread over sweet potatoes. Bake in 350°F (180°C) oven until heated through and topping starts to brown, about 30 minutes. Serves 8.

BAKED PORK CHOPS

After browning, these are cooked in the oven in a sauce. Tender.

Pork chops	16	16
Salt, sprinkle		
Pepper, sprinkle		
Medium onions, sliced	2	2
Large green pepper, cut matchstick size	1	1
Ketchup	1½ cups	375 mL
Brown sugar, packed	½ cup	125 mL
Prepared mustard	2 tbsp.	30 mL
Cinnamon	1 tsp.	5 mL
Ginger	1 tsp.	5 mL
Water	1 cup	250 mL

Trim excess fat from chops. Fry some fat in frying pan to grease pan. Brown chops on both sides. Sprinkle with salt and pepper. Transfer to roaster as they are browned.

Place onion and green pepper over chops in roaster.

Mix next 6 ingredients together in small bowl. Pour over all. Cover. Cook in 350°F (180°C) oven until fork tender, about 1½ hours. Makes 8 servings of 2 chops each.

United States

1. Bread Pudding page 148
   With Whiskey Sauce page 148
2. Hurricane page 135
3. Gumbo page 136
4. Jambalaya page 140
5. Creamed Spinach page 147
6. Creole Dressed Salad page 138

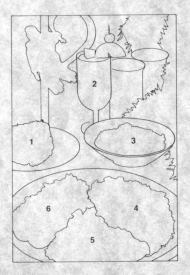

A creamy mixture with added chicken stuffing. Great taste.

Butter or margarine	¼ cup	50 mL
Fresh mushrooms, sliced	2 lbs.	900 g
Chopped onion	1 cup	250 mL
Condensed cream of mushroom soup	10 oz.	284 mL
Milk	1 cup	250 mL
Sherry (or alcohol-free sherry)	2 tbsp.	30 mL
Stuffing mix	6 oz.	170 g
Butter or margarine	2 tbsp.	30 mL

Melt first amount of butter in large frying pan. Add mushrooms and onion. Sauté for about 5 minutes. This will have to be done in 2 or 3 batches, adding more butter as needed.

Stir soup, milk and sherry together in bowl until smooth.

Put ½ mushroom-onion mixture into 2 quart (2.5 L) casserole. Mix seasoning packet and crumbs of stuffing mix together. Sprinkle ⅓ stuffing mix over mushrooms. Pour ½ soup-milk mixture over stuffing. Add layers of second half of mushrooms, ⅓ stuffing mix and second half of mushroom-milk mixture.

Melt remaining butter in small saucepan. Add remaining ⅓ stuffing mix. Stir. Sprinkle over top. Cover. Bake in 350°F (180°C) oven for about 40 minutes. Remove cover and bake another 5 to 10 minutes. Serves 8.

If a clock struck first you can't blame a person if he broke it to kill time.

Sliced chicken on toast covered with a cheese sauce. It's broiled then topped with bacon. A deep south favorite.

Large chicken breasts	4	4
Water	1 cup	250 mL
White bread slices, toasted and buttered	8	8
Bacon slices	16	16
SAUCE		
Butter or margarine	1/2 cup	125 mL
Finely chopped onion	1 cup	250 mL
All-purpose flour	1/2 cup	125 mL
Salt	1 tsp.	5 mL
Pepper	1/4 tsp.	1 mL
Milk	4 cups	1 L
Grated Parmesan cheese	1/3 cup	75 mL
Eggs, beaten	3	3
Grated Parmesan cheese, sprinkle		

Put the chicken breasts into small roaster. Add water. Cover and roast in 325°F (160°C) oven until tender, about 45 minutes to 1 hour. Pull meat off each side of breast in one chunk. Slice each to make 2 wide slices.

Place buttered toast in 200°F (110°C) oven to dry while preparing sauce. Spread out or offset a bit.

Fry bacon until crisp. Drain on paper towels. Place in oven on pan along with toast. Discard fat. Remove from oven just before increasing temperature for browning.

Sauce: Melt butter in frying pan. Add onion. Sauté until soft and clear.

Sprinkle flour, salt and pepper over onion. Mix. Add milk. Stir until it boils and thickens. Taste for salt and pepper, adding more if needed. Stir in first amount of Parmesan cheese. Add about 1/2 cup (125 mL) of sauce to eggs. Stir well. Now stir this mixture back into sauce, stirring constantly for almost 1 minute. Remove from heat.

(continued on next page)

To Assemble: Place 1 slice toast on tray. Crusts may be trimmed if you prefer. Lay 2 slices chicken (which is ½ chicken breast) on toast. Pour ½ cup (125 mL) sauce over chicken. Sprinkle with Parmesan cheese. Repeat for 7 more. Broil for 1 or 2 minutes until speckled brown. May also be put into 425°F (220°C) oven to brown. To serve, lay 2 slices bacon criss-cross fashion over each. Serves 8.

CREAMED SPINACH

Greens have always been a favorite in the south eastern United States.

Frozen chopped spinach	3 × 10 oz.	3 × 284 g
Boiling salted water		
Butter or margarine	⅓ cup	75 mL
All-purpose flour	⅓ cup	75 mL
Salt	1¼ tsp.	7 mL
Pepper	¼ tsp.	1 mL
Nutmeg, scant measure	¼ tsp.	1 mL
Milk	2½ cups	600 mL

Cook spinach in boiling salted water until thawed. Stir and cook about 2 minutes more. Drain thoroughly.

Melt butter in saucepan over medium heat. Mix in flour, salt, pepper and nutmeg. Stir in milk until it boils and thickens. Add spinach. Stir. Serves 8.

Pictured on page 143.

Paré Pointer

Mummies would never consider having a holiday in case they might relax and unwind.

BREAD PUDDING

A really good pudding that is a must for a New Orleans dessert as well as all of Louisiana.

Stale bread, cubed	4 cups	1 L
Milk	2 cups	500 mL
Eggs	3	3
Granulated sugar	1 cup	250 mL
Butter or margarine, melted	1/4 cup	50 mL
Fruit cocktail with juice	14 oz.	398 mL
Vanilla	2 tsp.	10 mL
Cinnamon	1 tsp.	5 mL
Raisins	1 cup	250 mL
Chopped pecans or walnuts (optional)	1/2 cup	125 mL
Long thread coconut	1/2 cup	125 mL

Combine first 10 ingredients in order given in mixing bowl. Let stand about 10 minutes so bread can absorb liquid. Mixture should be very soft but not like soup. Add a bit more liquid if necessary. Very dry bread will call for a bit more. Pour into greased 3 quart (4 L) casserole.

Scatter coconut over top. Bake in 350°F (180°C) oven for about 45 minutes until set and top is browned. Serve warm with Whiskey Sauce, below. Serves 8.

Pictured on page 143.

WHISKEY SAUCE

Make this traditional sauce before pudding is baked. It will be cooled when spooned over hot pudding. Small servings of this rich sauce are sufficient .

Butter or margarine	1/2 cup	125 mL
Granulated sugar	2 cups	500 mL
Eggs, beaten	2	2
Bourbon (or use water plus 2 tsp., 10 mL brandy flavoring)	1/4 cup	50 mL
Milk	1 cup	250 mL

(continued on next page)

Put butter and sugar into medium size saucepan over medium heat. Stir until melted and sugar is dissolved.

Remove from heat. Stir in beaten eggs. Add bourbon and milk and stir well. Sauce will thicken a bit when cooled. Spoon over hot pudding just before serving. Makes about 2 ⅔ cups (600 mL). Serves 8.

Pictured on page 143.

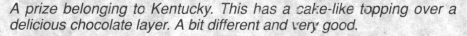

DERBY PIE.

A prize belonging to Kentucky. This has a cake-like topping over a delicious chocolate layer. A bit different and very good.

Butter or margarine, softened	¹/₂ cup	125 mL
Granulated sugar	1 cup	250 mL
Eggs	2	2
Bourbon	1 tbsp.	15 mL
Vanilla	1¹/₂ tsp.	7 mL
All-purpose flour	¹/₂ cup	125 mL
Salt	¹/₄ tsp.	1 mL
Semisweet chocolate chips	1 cup	250 mL
Chopped pecans	1 cup	250 mL
Unbaked pie shell, 9 inch (22 cm)	1	1
Whipped cream or ice cream		

Cream butter and sugar together in mixing bowl. Add eggs 1 at a time beating well after each addition. Add bourbon and vanilla, then add flour and salt. Beat until smooth.

Stir in chocolate chips and nuts.

Grease inside bottom of pie shell. Pour in filling. Bake on lowest shelf in 350°F (180°C) oven about 40 to 55 minutes until an inserted toothpick comes out clean. Makes 1 pie for 8 small servings. Make 2 pies for larger servings.

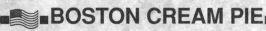# BOSTON CREAM PIE

It is worth a trip to Boston to have this dessert, served with tea of course.

CAKE
All-purpose flour	2 cups	450 mL
Granulated sugar	1 cup	225 mL
Baking powder	2½ tsp.	12 mL
Salt	1 tsp.	5 mL
Butter or margarine, softened	½ cup	125 mL
Milk	1 cup	225 mL
Egg	1	1
Vanilla	1 tsp.	5 mL

FILLING
Milk	1 cup	225 mL
Granulated sugar	¼ cup	50 mL
Cornstarch	2 tbsp.	30 mL
Egg	1	1
Vanilla	½ tsp.	2 mL

GLAZE
Icing (confectioner's) sugar	1 cup	250 mL
Cocoa	2 tbsp.	30 mL
Butter or margarine, melted	1 tbsp.	15 mL
Water	1 tbsp.	15 mL
Vanilla	¼ tsp.	1 mL

Cake: Measure all ingredients in order given into mixing bowl. Beat until smooth, about 2 to 3 minutes. Turn into 2 round greased 8 or 9 inch (20 or 22 cm) layer pans. Bake in 350°F (180°C) oven for about 25 minutes until an inserted pick comes out clean. Cool.

Filling: Bring milk to a boil in medium saucepan.

In small bowl mix sugar, cornstarch, egg and vanilla. Stir into boiling milk until it boils and thickens. Remove from heat. Cool. You can either use 1 or 2 cake layers. If using 1 layer, which is more common, slice in half to make 2 thin layers. Sandwich together with filling. Using 2 layers makes a larger dessert.

Glaze: Mix all 5 ingredients together in bowl. Add more water if needed to make a barely pourable glaze. Spread over top of cake. Allow a bit to run down the side here and there. Serves 8 with some left over.

Throughout this book measurements are given in Imperial and Metric measure. To compensate for differences between the two measurements due to rounding, a full metric measure is not always used.

The cup used is the standard 8 fluid ounce. Temperature is given n degrees Fahrenheit and Celsius. Baking Pan measurements are in inches and centimetres as well as quarts and litres. An exact conversion is given below as well as the working equivalent (Standard Measure).

IMPERIAL	METRIC	
	Exact Conversion	Standard Measure
Spoons	millilitre (mL)	millilitre (mL)
1/4 teaspoon (tsp.)	1.2 mL	1 mL
1/2 teaspoon (tsp.)	2.4 mL	2 mL
1 teaspoon (tsp.)	4.7 mL	5 mL
2 teaspoons (tsp.)	9.4 mL	10 mL
1 tablespoon (tbsp.)	14.2 mL	15 mL
Cups		
1/4 cup (4 tbsp.)	56.8 mL	50 mL
1/3 cup (5 1/3 tbsp.)	75.6 mL	75 mL
1/2 cup (8 tbsp.)	113.7 mL	125 mL
2/3 cup (10 2/3 tbsp.)	151.2 mL	150 mL
3/4 cup (12 tbsp.)	170.5 mL	175 mL
1 cup (16 tbsp.)	227.3 mL	250 mL
4 1/2 cups	984.8 mL	1000 mL, 1 litre (1 L)
Ounces (oz.)	**Grams (g)**	**Grams (g)**
1 oz.	28.3 g	30 g
2 oz.	56.7 g	55 g
3 oz.	85.0 g	85 g
4 oz.	113.4 g	125 g
5 oz.	141.7 g	140 g
6 oz.	170.1 g	170 g
7 oz.	198.4 g	200 g
8 oz.	226.8 g	250 g
16 oz.	453.6 g	500 g
32 oz.	917.2 g	1000 g, 1 kilogram (1 kg)

PANS, CASSEROLES

Imperial	Metric	Imperial	Metric
8x8 inch	20x20 cm	1 2/3 qt.	2 L
9x9 inch	22x22 cm	2 qt..	2.5 L
9x13 inch	22x33 cm	3 1/3 qt.	4 L
10x15 inch	25x38 cm	1 qt.	1.2 L
11x17 inch	28x43 cm	1 1/4 qt.	1.5 L
8x2 inch round	20x5 cm	1 2/3 qt.	2 L
9x2 inch round	22x5 cm	2 qt.	2.5 L
10x4 1/2 inch tube	25x11 cm	4 1/4 qt.	5 L
8x4x3 inch loaf	20x10x7 cm	1 1/4 qt.	1.5 L
9x5x3 inch loaf	23x12x7 cm	1 2/3 qt.	2 L

OVEN TEMPERATURES

Fahrenheit (°F)	Celsius (°C)
175°	80°
200°	100°
225°	110°
250°	120°
275°	140°
300°	150°
325°	160°
350°	180°
375°	190°
400°	200°
425°	220°
450°	230°
475°	240°
500°	260°

INDEX

COOKBOOKS

SAVE
$5.00!

COMPANY'S COMING
PUBLISHING LIMITED
BOX 8037, STATION "F"
EDMONTON, ALBERTA,
CANADA T6H 4N9

Please send the following cookbooks to the address on the reverse side of this coupon.

ENGLISH		
TITLE (Hard Cover @ $17.95 each)	**QUANTITY**	**AMOUNT**
JEAN PARÉ'S FAVORITES		
VOLUME ONE - 232 pages		
TITLE (Soft Cover @ $10.95 each)		
150 DELICIOUS SQUARES		
CASSEROLES		
MUFFINS & MORE		
SALADS		
APPETIZERS		
DESSERTS		
SOUPS & SANDWICHES		
HOLIDAY ENTERTAINING		
COOKIES		
VEGETABLES		
MAIN COURSES		
PASTA		
CAKES		
BARBECUES		
DINNERS OF THE WORLD		
(September, 1991)		
FRENCH		
TITLE (Soft Cover @ $10.95 each)		
150 DÉLICIEUX CARRÉS		
LES CASSEROLES		
MUFFINS ET PLUS		
TOTAL ALL BOOKS		$

■ **SAVE $5.00**

Order any 2 cookbooks by mail at regular prices and SAVE $5.00 on every third cookbook per order.

■ *Prices subject to change without prior notice.*

■ *Sorry, no C.O.D.'s*

■ **ORDERS OUTSIDE CANADA:**
Must be paid in U.S. funds by cheque or money order drawn on Canadian or U.S. bank.

■ **MAKE CHEQUE OR MONEY ORDER PAYABLE TO:**
COMPANY'S COMING PUBLISHING LIMITED

TOTAL COST OF BOOKS	$
LESS $5.00 for every third book per order	−
PLUS $1.50 postage & handling per book	+
SUB TOTAL	$
Canadian residents add GST	+
TOTAL AMOUNT ENCLOSED	$

↓   GIFT CARD MESSAGE   ↓

COOKBOOKS

A GIFT FOR YOU

COOKBOOKS

A NATIONAL BEST SELLER

I would like to order the Company's Coming Cookbooks listed on the reverse side of this coupon.

NAME_____
(PLEASE PRINT)

STREET_____

CITY _____

PROVINCE/STATE _____ POSTAL CODE/ZIP _____

GIFT GIVING – WE MAKE IT EASY...
... YOU MAKE IT DELICIOUS!

Let us help you with your gift giving! We will send cookbooks directly to the recipients of your choice if you give us their names and addresses. Be sure to specify the titles of the cookbooks you wish to send to each person.

Enclose a personal note or card for each gift or use our handy gift card below.

Company's Coming Cookbooks are the perfect gift for birthdays, showers, Mother's Day, Father's Day, graduation or any occasion ... collect them all!

Don't forget to take advantage of the **$5.00 saving ... buy any two Company's Coming Cookbooks by mail and save $5.00 on every third copy per order.**

↓   GIFT CARD MESSAGE   ↓

COMPANY'S COMING
PUBLISHING LIMITED
BOX 8037, STATION "F"
EDMONTON, ALBERTA,
CANADA T6H 4N9

COOKBOOKS

SAVE $5.00!

Please send the following cookbooks to the address on the reverse side of this coupon.

ENGLISH		
TITLE (Hard Cover @ $17.95 each)	QUANTITY	AMOUNT
JEAN PARÉ'S FAVORITES		
VOLUME ONE - 232 pages		
TITLE (Soft Cover @ $10.95 each)		
150 DELICIOUS SQUARES		
CASSEROLES		
MUFFINS & MORE		
SALADS		
APPETIZERS		
DESSERTS		
SOUPS & SANDWICHES		
HOLIDAY ENTERTAINING		
COOKIES		
VEGETABLES		
MAIN COURSES		
PASTA		
CAKES		
BARBECUES		
DINNERS OF THE WORLD		
(September, 1991)		

FRENCH		
TITLE (Soft Cover @ $10.95 each)		
150 DÉLICIEUX CARRÉS		
LES CASSEROLES		
MUFFINS ET PLUS		
TOTAL ALL BOOKS		$

- **SAVE $5.00**
  Order any 2 cookbooks by mail at regular prices and SAVE $5.00 on every third cookbook per order.

- *Prices subject to change without prior notice.*

- *Sorry, no C.O.D.'s*

- **ORDERS OUTSIDE CANADA:**
  Must be paid in U.S. funds by cheque or money order drawn on Canadian or U.S. bank.

- **MAKE CHEQUE OR MONEY ORDER PAYABLE TO:**
  COMPANY'S COMING PUBLISHING LIMITED

TOTAL COST OF BOOKS	$
LESS $5.00 for every third book per order	–
PLUS $1.50 postage & handling per book	+
SUB TOTAL	$
Canadian residents add GST	+
TOTAL AMOUNT ENCLOSED	$

↓   GIFT CARD MESSAGE   ↓

COOKBOOKS

A GIFT FOR YOU

COOKBOOKS ®

A NATIONAL **BEST SELLER**

I would like to order the Company's Coming Cookbooks listed on the reverse side of this coupon.

NAME_____
(PLEASE PRINT)

STREET_____

CITY _____

PROVINCE/STATE _____ POSTAL CODE/ZIP _____

GIFT GIVING – WE MAKE IT EASY...
... YOU MAKE IT DELICIOUS!

Let us help you with your gift giving! We will send cookbooks directly to the recipients of your choice if you give us their names and addresses. Be sure to specify the titles of the cookbooks you wish to send to each person.

Enclose a personal note or card for each gift or use our handy gift card below.

Company's Coming Cookbooks are the perfect gift for birthdays, showers, Mother's Day, Father's Day, graduation or any occasion ... collect them all!

Don't forget to take advantage of the **$5.00 saving ... buy any two Company's Coming Cookbooks by mail and save $5.00 on every third copy per order.**

↓ GIFT CARD MESSAGE ↓